The Evolution of Digital Asset Mining and Blockchain

Insights into Technological Innovation and Cryptocurrency Investment Strategies

Hyo Keom "Joseph" Kim

Joseph Kim holds an MBA, a Master's in Data Analytics, and a Bachelor's in Psychology.

He has led significant initiatives in blockchain, AI, and deep technology sectors throughout his career. As Chief Strategy Officer and Director at global technology companies, he has overseen the integration of advanced technologies, secured international investments, and guided full-scale business development projects.

In his role as Chairman of a Blockchain Association, Joseph has facilitated collaborations between the government, universities, and industry leaders to foster innovation within the blockchain ecosystem.

Additionally, he has led major projects in cryptocurrency mining, expanding both domestic and international infrastructure.

Email : jkyumc@gmail.com
Telegram : @Joseph_0210

COPYRIGHT

This is a work of creative nonfiction. Some parts have been fictionalized in varying degrees for various purposes.

All rights reserved. No part of this book may be reproduced in any form by any electronic or mechanical means, including information storage and retrieval systems, without permission in writing from the publisher, except by a reviewer who may quote brief passages in a review.

Copyright © Hyo Keom "Joseph" Kim, 2024

DISCLAIMER

This guide is intended for information and educational purposes only. In no event shall its authors, publishers, suppliers or partners be liable for any damages (including without limitation, damages for loss of data or profit, or due to business interruption) arising out of the use or inability to use the materials in this guide. Readers are advised to conduct their own research and due diligence and consult with a qualified professional before making any purchasing or financial decisions.

DISCLOSURE

This electronic version of this book may include hyperlinks to products and learning resources for reader convenience. The authors participate in various affiliate programs which may cover some of the tools and resources mentioned in this guide. This means they may earn a nominal fee on purchases from related partner websites.

TABLE OF CONTENTS

Introduction **10**

    I.   The Evolution of Blockchain and the Importance of Mining 11

    II. The Innovative Features of Blockchain Technology 14

    III. The History and Future Prospects of Cryptocurrency Mining 17

Chapter 1: The Technological Development of Blockchain and Consensus Algorithms **21**

    I.   The Basic Principles of Blockchain 21

    II. The Evolution of Consensus Algorithms 32

Chapter 2: Changes in Mining and Profit Realization **46**

    I.   Basic Principles of Mining 46

    II. Comparison of Mining Methods 56

    III. Various Mining Algorithms and Investment Opportunities 70

Chapter 3: Cryptocurrency Investment Strategies... 86

I. Understanding the Basics of Trading 86

II. Trading Strategies and Technical Analysis 96

III. Comparison of Long-term and Short-term Investment Strategies 110

Chapter 4: Growth and Prospects of the Cryptocurrency Market 122

I. Global Mining Market and Cryptocurrency Growth Rates 122

II. Eco-friendly Mining and Energy Consumption Issues 133

Chapter 5: Blockchain Regulations and Legal Issues.. 146

I. Current Status of Cryptocurrency Regulations in Various Countries 146

II. Legal Issues with Smart Contracts 160

III. Regulatory Directions for Investor Protection 171

Chapter 6: Data Analysis for Cryptocurrency Investment.. 182

    I.   Methods of Data Analysis in the Cryptocurrency Market..182

    II. Risk Management and Portfolio Optimization 194

Chapter 7: Business Applications of Blockchain Technology 207

    I.   Blockchain and Business Model Innovation....207

    II. Blockchain and ESG Investment 221

    III. Regulatory Response Strategies Using Data Analysis...234

    IV. Blockchain Adoption in Enterprises 245

Conclusion: The Future of Blockchain and Investment Strategies 258

    I.   Sustainability of Digital Asset Investments: Long-term Viability of Cryptocurrency Investments........259

II. Blockchain's Potential for Continuous Innovation: How Blockchain Technology Will Continue to Evolve 261

III. Integrating Mining and Trading for Profit Maximization: Strategies for Combining Mining and Trading Activities 264

IV. Future Cryptocurrency Market Opportunities: Insights into Emerging Opportunities within the Market.................................... 266

V. Impact of Technological Advancements on Investment: How Cutting-edge Technologies Will Influence the Investment Landscape. 268

Bibliography **271**

Glossary **274**

Introduction

The world of digital assets and decentralized technologies has undergone a profound transformation in recent years, spearheaded by the rise of blockchain technology and the revolutionary concept of cryptocurrency mining. What began as an obscure experiment in the digital sphere has now blossomed into a multibillion-dollar industry, reshaping traditional industries and unlocking new avenues for innovation, finance, and economic empowerment. At the core of this revolution lies blockchain technology, a decentralized ledger system that has revolutionized the way data is recorded, transactions are processed, and trust is established in a global network. Furthermore, cryptocurrency mining, a pivotal mechanism within blockchain ecosystems, plays a fundamental role in securing these networks and enabling the creation of new digital assets. In this introduction, we will explore the evolution of blockchain technology, the innovative features that make it a transformative force, and the history and future prospects of cryptocurrency mining as a driver of technological progress.

I. The Evolution of Blockchain and the Importance of Mining

Blockchain technology has evolved from its initial development as the underlying infrastructure for Bitcoin to a versatile platform with applications far beyond digital currencies. The concept of blockchain was first introduced in 2008 by an anonymous entity known as Satoshi Nakamoto, who created Bitcoin, the world's first cryptocurrency. Nakamoto's vision was to create a decentralized digital currency that could operate independently of centralized authorities, such as banks and governments. The key innovation that made this vision possible was blockchain—a distributed ledger system that allows for the secure, transparent, and immutable recording of transactions across a network of computers.

In the early days of blockchain, its primary application was limited to cryptocurrency transactions, with Bitcoin leading the charge. However, as the technology matured, developers and entrepreneurs began to recognize its potential to disrupt industries far beyond finance. Blockchain's decentralized nature, combined with its ability to provide transparency and security, has made it an attractive solution for industries such as supply chain management, healthcare, voting systems, and intellectual property. Companies are now using blockchain to enhance efficiency, reduce fraud, and improve accountability in processes that were previously vulnerable to corruption and inefficiencies.

One of the critical components that make blockchain ecosystems function is cryptocurrency mining. Mining is the process by which new blocks are added to the blockchain and transactions are validated. In essence, miners are responsible for maintaining the integrity and security of the blockchain network by solving complex mathematical problems that require significant computational power. When a miner successfully solves these problems, they are rewarded with newly minted cryptocurrency, such as Bitcoin. This process not only secures the network but also creates an incentive for individuals to contribute their computing resources to maintain the blockchain.

Mining serves as the backbone of many blockchain systems, ensuring that transactions are processed accurately and the network remains decentralized. Without miners, blockchain networks would be vulnerable to attacks, as there would be no mechanism to verify the legitimacy of transactions and prevent malicious actors from manipulating the system. Thus, mining is essential to the overall health and functionality of blockchain ecosystems, making it one of the most critical components of the digital asset economy.

As blockchain technology continues to evolve, so too does the role of mining. In the early days of Bitcoin, mining could be done using standard computers, but as the network grew, so did the complexity of the mathematical problems miners had to solve. This led to the development of specialized mining hardware, such as ASICs (Application-Specific Integrated Circuits), which are designed specifically for mining cryptocurrencies. Additionally, new consensus algorithms, such as Proof of Stake (PoS), are emerging as alternatives to the traditional Proof of Work (PoW) model used in Bitcoin, offering more energy-efficient ways to maintain blockchain networks.

II. The Innovative Features of Blockchain Technology

Blockchain technology has gained global recognition due to its innovative features that differentiate it from traditional systems of record-keeping and transactions. Three core attributes of blockchain—decentralization, transparency, and security—form the foundation of its appeal and have contributed to its widespread adoption.

- **Decentralization:** At the heart of blockchain is its decentralized nature. Unlike traditional systems where a single entity, such as a government or financial institution, controls data and transactions, blockchain operates on a distributed network of computers (known as nodes). Each node on the network maintains a copy of the entire blockchain, ensuring that no single entity has complete control over the system. This decentralization provides several benefits, including resilience against censorship, reduced risk of data tampering, and enhanced security. In the absence of a central authority, trust is established through consensus mechanisms, which ensure that all participants in the network agree on the validity of transactions.

- **Transparency:** One of the key selling points of blockchain is its transparency. Every transaction that occurs on a blockchain is recorded in a public ledger that is accessible to anyone with access to the network. This level of transparency provides a level of accountability that is unmatched by traditional systems. In industries such as supply chain management, for example, blockchain can provide real-time visibility into the movement of goods, ensuring that all parties have access to accurate and up-to-date information. Transparency also plays a critical role in reducing fraud and corruption, as all transactions are publicly visible and cannot be altered once they are recorded on the blockchain.

- **Security:** Security is another defining feature of blockchain technology. Each transaction that is added to the blockchain is secured using cryptographic algorithms, making it virtually impossible for anyone to alter the data without being detected. In addition, the decentralized nature of blockchain ensures that no single point of failure exists, as the data is replicated across multiple nodes in the network. This makes blockchain highly resistant to hacking and other forms of cyberattacks. The immutability of blockchain records also provides an additional layer of security, as once a transaction is added to the blockchain, it cannot be changed or deleted.

These innovative features have made blockchain a powerful tool for industries that require secure, transparent, and decentralized solutions. From financial services to healthcare and beyond, blockchain technology is reshaping the way businesses operate and interact with one another, offering new levels of efficiency, trust, and accountability.

III. The History and Future Prospects of Cryptocurrency Mining

The history of cryptocurrency mining is closely intertwined with the development of blockchain technology itself. In the early days of Bitcoin, mining was a relatively simple process that could be done using standard desktop computers. At the time, the Bitcoin network was small, and the computational power required to mine new blocks was minimal. However, as Bitcoin gained popularity and the number of transactions on the network increased, so did the difficulty of the mining process.

Over time, miners began to invest in more powerful hardware to increase their chances of solving the mathematical puzzles required to mine new blocks. This led to the rise of GPU (Graphics Processing Unit) mining, which provided a significant boost in computational power compared to standard CPUs. Eventually, specialized hardware known as ASICs became the industry standard for cryptocurrency mining, as they were specifically designed to perform the complex calculations required by the Bitcoin network.

The increasing complexity of mining has also led to concerns about its environmental impact. The energy consumption associated with cryptocurrency mining, particularly for PoW-based systems like Bitcoin, has become a significant issue. Bitcoin mining operations now consume as much electricity as entire countries, leading to widespread criticism from environmentalists and policymakers. This has prompted the development of more energy-efficient consensus mechanisms, such as Proof of Stake (PoS), which require less computational power to maintain the blockchain network.

Looking forward, the future of cryptocurrency mining is likely to be shaped by two key trends: the adoption of more sustainable practices and the continued evolution of mining technology. Efforts are already underway to reduce the environmental impact of mining by using renewable energy sources, such as solar and wind power. Additionally, new consensus algorithms, such as PoS and hybrid models, are gaining traction as more efficient alternatives to PoW.

As blockchain technology continues to evolve, the role of mining will also change. While PoW mining will likely remain a key component of certain blockchain networks, the shift towards more sustainable and scalable solutions will drive innovation in the mining industry. In the future, we may see the development of new mining algorithms that are less resource-intensive, as well as the integration of artificial intelligence and machine learning to optimize mining processes.

Chapter 1: The Technological Development of Blockchain and Consensus Algorithms

I. The Basic Principles of Blockchain

Blockchain technology is often described as one of the most revolutionary innovations of the 21st century, with the potential to transform industries from finance and healthcare to logistics and governance. At the heart of this innovation are several core principles, the most important of which are distributed ledger technology (DLT) and decentralization. These principles enable blockchain to offer enhanced transparency, security, and reliability without requiring centralized control. In this section, we will explore how blockchain achieves these benefits, beginning with a detailed explanation of distributed ledger technology and decentralization, followed by a technical breakdown of the structure of blockchain and the transaction validation process.

1. Distributed Ledger Technology and Decentralization

At its core, blockchain is a type of distributed ledger technology (DLT), a digital system for recording transactions across multiple locations or entities. Unlike traditional ledgers, which are typically managed by a single central authority (such as a bank or government agency), distributed ledgers do not rely on a central intermediary. Instead, they operate across a network of computers, or nodes, each of which maintains its own copy of the ledger. This decentralized structure is one of blockchain's most innovative and transformative features.

How Blockchain Ensures Transparency

One of the primary advantages of using DLT in a blockchain system is its ability to provide transparency. In traditional systems, a central authority maintains control over data, and access to that data is often limited or opaque. This creates the potential for information asymmetry, where the central authority has more information than other parties, which can lead to mistrust or inefficiencies.

Blockchain, however, operates in an entirely different manner. All transactions and data entries on a blockchain are recorded on a public ledger that is visible to every participant in the network. Each node, or participant, has access to the same version of the ledger, ensuring that all parties have an identical record of events. This transparency allows participants to verify transactions independently, creating a level of trust that does not depend on a central authority.

For example, in the financial industry, blockchain can be used to track the movement of assets or currency. Each transaction is visible to all participants, ensuring that no single party can manipulate the system without being detected. This transparency reduces the need for intermediaries like banks, as participants can trust the validity of the transactions by relying on the blockchain's distributed ledger.

How Blockchain Ensures Security Without Centralized Control

Decentralization is another key principle of blockchain technology. In traditional systems, a central authority is responsible for securing and maintaining the integrity of the system. However, this centralization creates a single point of failure, meaning that if the central authority is compromised, the entire system can be at risk. Additionally, centralized systems are vulnerable to censorship and manipulation, as the entity in control has the power to alter or block transactions.

Blockchain addresses these challenges through decentralization, distributing control and decision-making across a network of nodes. Rather than relying on a single authority to validate transactions and maintain security, blockchain uses consensus mechanisms to ensure that the majority of nodes in the network agree on the validity of transactions. This process of collective agreement, or consensus, helps to prevent fraud and unauthorized changes to the ledger.

One of the most widely used consensus mechanisms is Proof of Work (PoW), which is the foundation of Bitcoin's blockchain. In a PoW system, miners (nodes that perform the task of validating transactions) compete to solve complex cryptographic puzzles. The first miner to solve the puzzle earns the right to validate the block of transactions and add it to the blockchain. The solution to the puzzle is shared with the rest of the network, and once a majority of nodes agree that the solution is correct, the block is confirmed, and the transactions are considered valid. This process ensures that all participants have a shared and verified record of events without the need for centralized control.

Proof of Stake (PoS) is another consensus mechanism that provides an alternative to PoW. In a PoS system, validators (participants who have a stake in the network) are chosen to validate transactions based on the amount of cryptocurrency they hold. This reduces the energy consumption associated with PoW while maintaining security through decentralization. By distributing control across a broad network of participants, blockchain creates a secure environment where the integrity of the system is maintained by collective agreement rather than central authority.

2. The Structure of Blockchain and Transaction Process

Now that we have a basic understanding of the principles of distributed ledger technology and decentralization, let us dive deeper into the technical structure of blockchain and the process by which transactions are validated. At a high level, blockchain can be thought of as a series of blocks, each of which contains a list of transactions. These blocks are linked together in a chain, creating an immutable and chronological record of all transactions that have ever occurred on the network.

The Structure of a Block

Each block in a blockchain consists of several components, including the following:

- **Header:** The header contains metadata about the block, such as its unique dentifier (hash), the timestamp of when it was created, and the hash of the previous block in the chain. The inclusion of the previous block's hash ensures that each block is linked to the one before it, forming a chain of blocks.
- **Transactions:** The body of the block contains a list of transactions that have been grouped together for validation. Each transaction records a specific action, such as the transfer of cryptocurrency from one account to another.
- **Merkle Tree Root:** The Merkle tree root is a cryptographic structure that ensures the integrity of the transactions within the block. It works by creating a tree-like structure where each transaction is hashed, and the resulting hashes are combined to create a single root hash. This root hash is included in the block header, providing a way to verify the validity of the transactions without storing all the individual transaction data.

- **Nonce (in PoW systems):** A nonce is a random number used in Proof of Work systems to ensure that miners must expend computational effort to find a valid block. The miner repeatedly changes the nonce value and recalculates the block's hash until the resulting hash meets the network's difficulty requirements.

The Process of Adding a Block to the Blockchain

The process of adding a new block to the blockchain begins when a transaction is initiated. For example, in a cryptocurrency blockchain like Bitcoin, a user might want to send Bitcoin to another user. The following steps outline the transaction process:

- **Transaction Broadcast**

   The transaction is broadcast to the network, where it is received by nodes (miners or validators) that participate in the transaction validation process.

- **Transaction Validation**

   Before a transaction can be added to the blockchain, it must be validated. Validation involves ensuring that the user initiating the transaction has the necessary funds to complete the transfer and that the transaction adheres to the rules of the network (e.g., the correct format, proper signatures).

- **Inclusion in a Block**

    Once a transaction is validated, it is grouped together with other transactions in a block. In PoW systems, miners compete to solve a cryptographic puzzle (the Proof of Work) to earn the right to add the block to the blockchain.

- **Consensus Mechanism**

    The consensus mechanism ensures that the majority of nodes in the network agree on the validity of the new block. In PoW systems, this is done by verifying the miner's solution to the cryptographic puzzle. In PoS systems, validators must prove they have a stake in the network to participate in the validation process.

- **Block Addition**

    Once consensus is reached, the new block is added to the blockchain. The block's header contains the hash of the previous block, linking the new block to the existing chain and ensuring the immutability of the record.

- **Propagation Across the Network**

    After the new block is added to the blockchain, it is propagated across the network. Each node updates its copy of the blockchain to include the new block, ensuring that all participants have the same version of the ledger.

- **Transaction Confirmation**

    Once the block containing the transaction is added to the blockchain, the transaction is considered confirmed. In most blockchain networks, a transaction is deemed fully confirmed after several additional blocks are added to the chain, further securing the transaction's position in the ledger.

The Role of Hashing and Cryptography in Blockchain

A crucial component of blockchain's security and functionality is its use of cryptographic hashing. A hash is a unique fixed-length string of characters generated from input data of any size. In the context of blockchain, hashing is used to generate unique identifiers for blocks and transactions. Hashes play a critical role in ensuring the immutability of blockchain records. Once a block is added to the chain, any change to the data within that block would result in a completely different hash, immediately alerting the network to the alteration.

Blockchain relies on public-key cryptography to secure transactions. Each participant in the network has a pair of cryptographic keys: a public key (which acts as an address that others can use to send transactions) and a private key (which is used to sign transactions and prove ownership). This ensures that only the rightful owner of a cryptocurrency can authorize its transfer, providing a high level of security.

II. The Evolution of Consensus Algorithms

Blockchain technology has become one of the most transformative innovations of the 21st century, largely due to its ability to offer secure, decentralized, and immutable systems without the need for centralized intermediaries. The foundation of this security and decentralization lies in the consensus mechanisms that allow a network of participants to agree on the validity of transactions. The two most widely used consensus algorithms in the blockchain ecosystem are Proof of Work (PoW) and Proof of Stake (PoS). In recent years, new technologies, such as Zero-Knowledge Proofs (ZKPs), have also emerged, further enhancing the privacy, efficiency, and scalability of blockchain systems. This section explores the evolution of consensus algorithms, comparing PoW and PoS, examining the role of ZKPs, and predicting the future of consensus mechanisms.

1. Comparison Between PoW (Proof of Work) and PoS (Proof of Stake)

Proof of Work (PoW)

Proof of Work (PoW) is the original consensus algorithm and the foundation of the first blockchain system, Bitcoin. Introduced by Bitcoin's pseudonymous creator Satoshi Nakamoto in 2008, PoW was designed to solve the double-spending problem in decentralized networks, ensuring that participants could not spend the same unit of cryptocurrency twice.

At its core, PoW requires network participants, known as miners, to compete to solve complex cryptographic puzzles. These puzzles require significant computational power and energy to solve. The first miner to solve the puzzle earns the right to validate a new block of transactions and add it to the blockchain. In return for their effort, the winning miner receives a block reward, usually in the form of cryptocurrency (e.g., Bitcoin).

The PoW algorithm ensures that blocks are added to the blockchain at a steady rate. For Bitcoin, this rate is approximately one block every 10 minutes. Once a block is added, it becomes nearly impossible to alter it without redoing the computational work for all subsequent blocks, ensuring the immutability of the blockchain.

Advantages of PoW

- **Security:** PoW provides a high level of security. The computational effort required to solve the puzzles makes it extremely difficult for any single entity to gain control of the network, a concept known as a 51% attack. To alter the blockchain, an attacker would need to control more than half of the network's total computational power, which is prohibitively expensive for large blockchain networks like Bitcoin.
- **Proven Track Record:** Bitcoin, the first blockchain using PoW, has been operational since 2009

without major security breaches, demonstrating the effectiveness of the PoW mechanism.

Disadvantages of PoW

- **Energy Consumption:** One of the most significant drawbacks of PoW is its energy consumption. Miners must use powerful hardware to solve puzzles, leading to massive energy usage. For instance, the Bitcoin network consumes more electricity than some entire countries, raising concerns about the environmental sustainability of PoW.
- **Centralization of Mining Power:** Although PoW is designed to be decentralized, in practice, mining power has become concentrated in regions with low electricity costs and in the hands of large mining pools. This undermines the decentralization that blockchain aims to achieve.
- **Scalability:** PoW-based networks face scalability issues due to the time and energy required to add each block to the chain. The throughput (number

of transactions per second) is relatively low compared to traditional payment systems like Visa.

Proof of Stake (PoS)

Proof of Stake (PoS) was introduced as an alternative consensus mechanism to address some of the challenges posed by PoW, especially its energy consumption. Rather than requiring miners to solve computational puzzles, PoS allows validators (sometimes called "stakers") to validate new blocks based on the amount of cryptocurrency they hold (i.e., their "stake"). The more tokens a validator holds, the higher their chances of being selected to validate the next block.

Validators in a PoS system do not compete in the same way that miners in a PoW system do. Instead, the selection process is typically random but weighted by the size of the stake. Validators are incentivized to act honestly because they stand to lose part of their staked assets if they attempt to validate fraudulent transactions (this is called "slashing"). After a block is validated, it is added to the blockchain, and the validator receives a reward in cryptocurrency.

Advantages of PoS

- **Energy Efficiency:** One of the primary advantages of PoS over PoW is its energy efficiency. Since PoS does not require validators to solve computational puzzles, it consumes far less energy, making it a more sustainable and environmentally friendly consensus mechanism.

- **Lower Entry Barriers:** PoS allows a broader range of participants to engage in the validation process because it does not require specialized and expensive hardware. Anyone with a sufficient stake in the network can become a validator.

- **Decentralization:** By lowering the cost and energy requirements for participating in the validation process, PoS encourages broader participation and can enhance decentralization compared to PoW.

Disadvantages of PoS

- **Wealth Concentration:** In PoS systems, validators are selected based on the size of their stake, which can lead to the concentration of power among the wealthiest participants. Those who hold large amounts of cryptocurrency have a higher chance of being selected as validators and receiving rewards, further increasing their wealth over time.
- **Security Concerns:** Although PoS is designed to be secure, it is relatively new compared to PoW and has not been tested at the same scale. Some critics argue that PoS systems may be more vulnerable to certain attacks, such as "long-range attacks" or "nothing-at-stake" attacks.

PoW vs. PoS: A Summary Comparison

Feature	Proof of Work (PoW)	Proof of Stake (PoS)
Energy Consumption	High	Low
Security	Proven security over time	Newer, less tested at scale
Decentralization	Mining power concentrated in regions	Potential for wealth concentration
Scalability	Limited by computational effort	More scalable than PoW
Participation Barriers	Requires expensive hardware	Open to anyone with a sufficient stake

2. The Emergence and Role of Zero-Knowledge Proof Technology

As blockchain technology continues to evolve, new techniques are being developed to enhance its functionality, particularly in the areas of privacy and scalability. One of the most promising of these techniques is Zero-Knowledge Proof (ZKP) technology.

What Are Zero-Knowledge Proofs?

A zero-knowledge proof is a cryptographic method that allows one party (the "prover") to prove to another party (the "verifier") that a certain statement is true, without revealing any information beyond the fact that the statement is true. In other words, zero-knowledge proofs enable participants to verify the correctness of information without exposing the underlying data.

In the context of blockchain, ZKPs can be used to enhance privacy by allowing participants to validate transactions without revealing details such as the sender's address, the recipient's address, or the transaction amount. This has significant implications for privacy-focused blockchain networks, where users want to maintain confidentiality while still ensuring the integrity of the blockchain.

Applications of Zero-Knowledge Proofs in Blockchain

- **Privacy:** One of the most important applications of ZKPs is in privacy-preserving blockchains. For example, Zcash, a privacy-focused cryptocurrency, uses a form of ZKP called zk-SNARKs (Zero-Knowledge Succinct Non-Interactive Arguments of Knowledge) to enable private transactions. ZKPs allow users to verify the validity of transactions without revealing the details, offering enhanced privacy while maintaining the security of the network.
- **Scalability:** ZKPs also have the potential to improve the scalability of blockchain networks. For example, zk-rollups, a layer 2 scaling solution for Ethereum, use ZKPs to batch multiple transactions into a single proof. This reduces the amount of

data that needs to be stored on-chain, allowing the network to process more transactions per second. By minimizing the computational and storage requirements for verifying transactions, zk-rollups can significantly enhance blockchain scalability.

- **Interoperability:** ZKPs can also facilitate interoperability between different blockchain networks. For example, zero-knowledge proofs can be used to verify cross-chain transactions without revealing sensitive information, allowing assets to be transferred securely between different blockchain platforms.

3. The Future of Consensus Algorithms

As blockchain technology continues to evolve, new consensus algorithms are being developed to address the limitations of PoW and PoS and to improve the scalability, security, and efficiency of blockchain networks. Some of the most promising emerging consensus mechanisms include:

Delegated Proof of Stake (DPoS)

Delegated Proof of Stake (DPoS) is a variation of PoS designed to enhance scalability and decentralization. In a DPoS system, token holders elect a small group of delegates to validate transactions and create new blocks. These delegates are responsible for maintaining the network's integrity, and they can be voted out by the community if they fail to act in the best interests of the network.

DPoS offers several advantages, including higher transaction throughput and faster block confirmation times compared to traditional PoW and PoS systems. However, it has also faced criticism for concentrating power in the hands of a small group of delegates, potentially undermining decentralization.

Proof of Authority (PoA)

Proof of Authority (PoA) is a consensus algorithm that replaces miners or validators with a group of pre-approved, trusted nodes. These nodes, or authorities, are responsible for validating transactions and maintaining the blockchain. PoA is often used in private or consortium blockchains, where trust between participants is already established, and high throughput is a priority.

While PoA offers significant scalability and efficiency advantages, it sacrifices decentralization, making it less suitable for public blockchains that prioritize trustlessness.

Proof of History (PoH)

Proof of History (PoH) is a consensus mechanism used by the Solana blockchain that provides a historical record of events to improve scalability and transaction speed. PoH uses a verifiable delay function (VDF) to create a cryptographic timestamp for each transaction. This allows validators to process transactions more efficiently without waiting for global consensus, enabling Solana to achieve high throughput and low transaction latency.

Byzantine Fault Tolerance (BFT)

Byzantine Fault Tolerance (BFT) is a class of consensus algorithms designed to protect against Byzantine faults, where participants in the network act maliciously or unpredictably. BFT algorithms enable a blockchain network to reach consensus even in the presence of faulty or malicious nodes. Practical Byzantine Fault Tolerance (PBFT) and Tendermint are two examples of BFT-based consensus mechanisms used in blockchain systems.

BFT algorithms are particularly well-suited for permissioned or consortium blockchains, where a known set of participants operate the network.

Chapter 2: Changes in Mining and Profit Realization

I. Basic Principles of Mining

1. The Process and Principles of Cryptocurrency Mining

Cryptocurrency mining is a crucial component of blockchain technology, particularly in Proof of Work (PoW) consensus algorithms. It ensures the integrity and security of decentralized networks, allowing transactions to be verified and recorded without a central authority. The mining process involves solving complex mathematical problems to validate blocks of transactions, which are then added to the blockchain. Miners are incentivized for their work through the reward of newly created cryptocurrency, such as Bitcoin, or transaction fees.

To understand cryptocurrency mining, it's essential to break down the process into several key steps:

- **Transaction Initiation:** A transaction on a cryptocurrency network begins when a user initiates a transfer of digital assets, such as Bitcoin, to another user. This transaction is broadcast to the network, where it waits in a pool of unconfirmed transactions known as the mempool. At this stage, the transaction is yet to be validated or included in the blockchain.
- **Transaction Aggregation into Blocks:** Miners collect pending transactions from the mempool and aggregate them into a block. A block is essentially a container that holds a group of verified transactions, along with critical information such as the previous block's hash, a timestamp, and a unique identifier known as a nonce.
- **Hashing and Block Validation:** The primary function of miners is to solve a complex cryptographic puzzle, which is part of the PoW consensus mechanism. This puzzle involves finding a specific hash value that matches a

predefined condition (known as the target difficulty). A hash is a fixed-length alphanumeric string produced by a cryptographic function that converts an input (in this case, the block's data) into a seemingly random output. The objective is to modify the nonce, the unique identifier in the block header, until the hash of the block's contents meets the required difficulty level.The difficulty target is adjusted regularly by the network to ensure that blocks are mined at a consistent rate. For Bitcoin, for example, the network aims to have a new block mined approximately every 10 minutes. If blocks are being mined too quickly or too slowly, the network adjusts the difficulty of the cryptographic puzzle accordingly.

- **Proof of Work and Consensus:** Once a miner finds the correct hash value, they broadcast the newly validated block to the network. Other nodes (computers) on the network quickly verify the block's legitimacy by checking if the hash meets the target difficulty. If the block is valid, it is added to the blockchain, and the miner is rewarded with newly minted cryptocurrency and any transaction fees associated with the transactions included in the block. This process is competitive, as numerous miners are racing to solve the cryptographic puzzle first. Only the miner who finds the correct solution first gets the reward, which incentivizes miners to invest in more powerful hardware to increase their chances of success. However, once a block is added to the blockchain, it becomes part of a permanent and immutable ledger, ensuring the system's integrity.

- **Block Propagation:** After a block is validated and added to the blockchain, it is propagated throughout the network. Each node in the network updates its copy of the blockchain to reflect the newly added block. This propagation ensures that all participants in the network have an identical copy of the ledger, reinforcing the decentralized nature of the system.

2. Energy Consumption and Environmental Problems in Mining

While cryptocurrency mining is vital to the functioning of blockchain networks, it has been increasingly criticized for its significant energy consumption and environmental impact. Mining, particularly in PoW systems, is an energy-intensive process due to the computational power required to solve cryptographic puzzles.

Energy Consumption in PoW Mining

The energy consumption associated with mining comes primarily from the computational resources needed to perform the hashing process. As miners solve cryptographic puzzles, they rely on powerful hardware to run millions of computations per second. The most common hardware used for mining includes:

- **Central Processing Units (CPUs):** While CPUs were once sufficient for early cryptocurrency mining, they are now largely obsolete due to their relatively low processing power.

- **Graphics Processing Units (GPUs):** GPUs, often found in gaming computers, are better suited for mining because they can perform many calculations simultaneously, making them more efficient than CPUs for tasks like hashing.
- **Application-Specific Integrated Circuits (ASICs):** ASICs are highly specialized mining devices designed to perform a specific function, such as solving the cryptographic puzzles used in Bitcoin mining. ASICs are far more efficient than both CPUs and GPUs, making them the preferred choice for large-scale mining operations.

As mining hardware has become more powerful, the difficulty of mining has increased, requiring even more computational power to mine blocks. This escalation in computing power has led to a corresponding increase in electricity consumption. A report by the University of Cambridge estimated that the Bitcoin network alone consumes more electricity annually than some small countries, such as Argentina or the Netherlands.

Environmental Impact

The environmental impact of cryptocurrency mining arises primarily from the high energy demands, much of which is sourced from non-renewable energy such as coal and natural gas. The more energy-intensive the mining process, the higher the carbon emissions associated with it. The following are the key environmental concerns related to mining:

- **Carbon Footprint:** A significant portion of the electricity used in mining comes from fossil fuel-based power plants, contributing to greenhouse gas emissions and exacerbating climate change. Large mining operations in countries with cheap electricity, such as China (before its mining ban) or Kazakhstan, often rely on coal-powered plants, which have a high carbon footprint.
- **E-Waste:** The mining hardware itself poses an environmental challenge. ASIC miners, for example,

become obsolete relatively quickly as newer, more efficient models are developed. This rapid turnover in hardware creates a significant amount of electronic waste (e-waste). Given the specialized nature of ASICs, they cannot be repurposed for other tasks, meaning that obsolete hardware is often discarded, contributing to the growing global e-waste problem.

- **Water Consumption:** In addition to electricity, some mining operations rely on water for cooling their hardware. This can strain local water resources, particularly in regions where water is scarce. The competition for natural resources can create tension between mining operations and local communities.

Environmental Solutions and Alternatives

Recognizing the environmental challenges posed by mining, there has been increasing interest in developing more sustainable mining practices and alternative consensus mechanisms to PoW.

- **Transition to Renewable Energy:** One approach to mitigating the environmental impact of mining is to power operations using renewable energy sources, such as solar, wind, and hydroelectric power. Iceland, for instance, has become a popular location for mining due to its abundant geothermal energy. By shifting to renewable energy, mining operations can significantly reduce their carbon footprint.
- **Proof of Stake (PoS) and Other Consensus Mechanisms:** One of the most promising alternatives to PoW is Proof of Stake (PoS), which eliminates the need for energy-intensive mining. In a PoS system, validators are chosen to create new blocks and confirm transactions based on the number of coins they hold and are willing to "stake" as collateral. PoS requires far less computational power and energy, making it a more environmentally friendly option. Ethereum, the second-largest cryptocurrency by market capitalization, has recently transitioned from PoW

to PoS with the Ethereum 2.0 upgrade, a move expected to reduce its energy consumption by over 99%.

- **Energy-Efficient Algorithms:** Another solution is the development of more energy-efficient mining algorithms. For example, newer cryptocurrencies like Chia use a Proof of Space and Time (PoST) consensus mechanism, which relies on hard drive space rather than computational power. This reduces the energy required to maintain the network while still ensuring security and decentralization.

Regulatory and Industry Responses

Governments and regulatory bodies are increasingly scrutinizing the environmental impact of cryptocurrency mining. Some countries, such as China, have implemented outright bans on mining due to concerns over energy consumption and its effect on carbon emissions. Other nations are introducing stricter regulations, encouraging mining operations to adopt cleaner energy sources.

Industry initiatives are also gaining traction. The *Crypto Climate Accord*, for instance, is a private-sector initiative aimed at achieving net-zero emissions for the cryptocurrency industry by 2040. The accord encourages mining operations to transition to renewable energy and promotes research into greener consensus mechanisms.

II. Comparison of Mining Methods

Cryptocurrency mining is essential for validating transactions and securing decentralized networks, particularly in blockchain ecosystems. The three main hardware-based methods for mining—CPU, GPU, and ASIC mining—differ significantly in terms of efficiency, profitability, accessibility, and environmental impact. Additionally, the shift from Proof of Work (PoW) to Proof of Stake (PoS) mining has altered the landscape of cryptocurrency mining, with each consensus mechanism offering distinct approaches to validating transactions and generating rewards.

1. Advantages and Disadvantages of CPU, GPU, and ASIC Mining

Each of the primary mining methods—using Central Processing Units (CPUs), Graphics Processing Units (GPUs), and Application-Specific Integrated Circuits (ASICs)—has distinct advantages and disadvantages. These differences are critical in determining the most suitable mining method for specific cryptocurrencies, depending on the balance between efficiency and profitability.

CPU Mining

Advantages:

- **Accessibility:** CPU mining was the earliest form of mining and is easily accessible. Nearly anyone with a computer can participate in CPU mining without investing in specialized equipment. This makes it a more democratic entry point for individuals looking to get involved in cryptocurrency mining.

- **Low Initial Investment:** Since every computer already contains a CPU, the initial cost of getting started with CPU mining is relatively low. Miners do not need to purchase additional hardware, making it an appealing option for hobbyists or those who want to mine on a small scale.
- **Flexibility:** CPUs are general-purpose processors, meaning they can perform a wide variety of tasks. In addition to mining, they can run other software, making them versatile components in a mining setup.

Disadvantages:

- **Low Efficiency:** The biggest downside of CPU mining is its inefficiency compared to other methods. CPUs can process only a limited number of calculations per second, making them ineffective for mining popular cryptocurrencies like Bitcoin, which now require immense computational power to remain competitive.

- **Low Profitability:** Given their slow speed and low efficiency, CPU miners generally earn less in rewards The time and energy consumed often outweigh the potential profits, especially when mining larger, more competitive cryptocurrencies.
- **Unsuitability for Major Cryptocurrencies:** Due to the rise of more powerful mining methods like GPU and ASIC mining, CPUs are no longer viable for mining mainstream cryptocurrencies like Bitcoin or Ethereum. Most modern blockchains either require higher processing power or have moved to consensus algorithms that discourage CPU mining.

CPU Mining Use Cases:

Despite its inefficiency for large networks, CPU mining can still be effective for mining smaller, less popular cryptocurrencies, also known as altcoins.

Cryptocurrencies like Monero, which use algorithms specifically designed to resist ASIC mining, offer a niche market for CPU miners.

GPU Mining

Advantages:

- **Higher Efficiency Compared to CPUs:** GPUs are designed to handle complex mathematical operations simultaneously, making them more efficient at solving the cryptographic puzzles involved in PoW mining. A single GPU can outperform multiple CPUs in mining speed and efficiency.
- **Versatility Across Cryptocurrencies:** GPUs are more versatile than ASICs, allowing miners to mine a wide variety of cryptocurrencies without the need for specialized hardware. This adaptability allows GPU miners to switch between different coins as market conditions change.
- **Relatively Affordable Entry Point:** While more expensive than CPUs, GPUs are still relatively

affordable, especially compared to ASICs. This makes GPU mining more accessible to small-scale miners who want to participate in cryptocurrency mining without a large upfront investment.

Disadvantages:

- **Energy Consumption:** GPU mining is more energy-efficient than CPU mining, but it still consumes considerable amounts of electricity, especially when multiple GPUs are used in mining rigs. This can lead to higher operational costs, which reduce profitability.
- **Lower Profitability Compared to ASICs:** While GPUs offer better efficiency than CPUs, they are generally less profitable than ASICs for mining major cryptocurrencies like Bitcoin. As mining difficulty increases, GPUs struggle to keep up with ASIC hardware.
- **Hardware Degradation:** The intense workload involved in mining can lead to faster degradation of GPUs compared to CPUs. This necessitates more frequent hardware upgrades or

replacements, increasing overall operational costs over time.

GPU Mining Use Cases:

- GPUs are especially well-suited for mining cryptocurrencies that use algorithms resistant to ASIC mining, such as Ethereum (prior to its shift to PoS), Ravencoin, and Zcash. These cryptocurrencies favor parallel processing power, making GPUs a more profitable choice.

ASIC Mining

Advantages:

- **Highest Efficiency and Processing Power:** ASICs are custom-built for cryptocurrency mining, specifically designed to handle the computational tasks required for solving PoW cryptographic puzzles. They offer significantly higher processing power than both CPUs and GPUs, making them the most efficient hardware for mining popular cryptocurrencies like Bitcoin.

- **Increased Profitability:** Due to their superior computational power, ASIC miners can solve puzzles faster, increasing the likelihood of successfully mining a block and earning rewards. This makes ASIC mining far more profitable than CPU and GPU mining, particularly for large-scale operations.
- **Longevity for Specific Cryptocurrencies:** ASICs are designed to mine specific cryptocurrencies, which allows them to operate at peak efficiency for those coins. Bitcoin ASICs, for example, are highly optimized for the SHA-256 algorithm used in Bitcoin mining.

Disadvantages:
- High Initial Investment: ASICs are expensive, often costing thousands of dollars per unit. This high upfront cost can be prohibitive for individual miners or small-scale operations, making ASIC

mining more accessible to large, well-funded operations.

- **Lack of Flexibility:** ASICs are built to mine specific algorithms, meaning that they can only mine a narrow range of cryptocurrencies. If a miner wants to switch to a different cryptocurrency, they would need to invest in a new ASIC for that coin's specific algorithm.
- **Energy Consumption:** ASICs are the most energy-intensive mining hardware, requiring significant amounts of electricity to function. This results in higher operational costs and contributes to environmental concerns related to cryptocurrency mining.
- **Obsolescence:** As mining difficulty increases and new ASIC models are developed, older ASICs quickly become obsolete. This forces miners to upgrade their hardware regularly to remain competitive, adding to the overall cost of ASIC mining.

ASIC Mining Use Cases:

ASIC mining is ideal for large-scale operations focused on major cryptocurrencies like Bitcoin and Litecoin. These coins use algorithms that favor ASICs, making this method the most profitable for mining dominant blockchain networks.

2. Differences Between Proof of Work (PoW) and Proof of Stake (PoS) Mining

As cryptocurrency mining has evolved, so too have the consensus mechanisms that underpin blockchain networks. The two most prominent mechanisms are Proof of Work (PoW) and Proof of Stake (PoS). Each has a unique impact on the mining process, efficiency, profitability, and the overall sustainability of the blockchain.

Proof of Work (PoW) Mining

PoW is the original consensus mechanism used in blockchain networks like Bitcoin and, until recently,

Ethereum. It requires miners to compete to solve complex mathematical puzzles, with the first to find the correct solution earning the right to add a new block to the blockchain. The rewards come in the form of newly created coins and transaction fees.

Advantages of PoW Mining:

- **Security and Decentralization:** PoW mining is highly secure due to the enormous computational power required to attack the network. The more miners participate, the harder it is for any single entity to control the network, ensuring decentralization.
- **Established Mechanism:** PoW has been tested and proven over more than a decade, making it a trusted method for securing blockchain networks. Its use in Bitcoin, the most valuable cryptocurrency, has solidified its place in the ecosystem.

Disadvantages of PoW Mining:

- **Energy Consumption:** One of the most significant criticisms of PoW is its energy-intensive nature. Mining requires vast amounts of computational power, leading to high electricity consumption. This has raised concerns about the environmental impact of PoW mining.
- **Mining Centralization:** Over time, PoW mining has become dominated by large mining farms with access to specialized hardware and cheap electricity. This centralization undermines the decentralized ethos of blockchain and reduces opportunities for smaller participants.

Profitability in PoW Mining:

Profitability in PoW mining is heavily influenced by the price of the cryptocurrency being mined, the efficiency of the hardware used, and the cost of electricity. ASIC miners tend to be the most profitable for PoW mining, especially for cryptocurrencies like Bitcoin.

Proof of Stake (PoS) Mining

PoS, an alternative to PoW, eliminates the need for energy-intensive mining. Instead, validators are chosen to create new blocks and confirm transactions based on the number of coins they hold and are willing to "stake" as collateral. Validators earn rewards based on the amount they stake, as opposed to competing with others to solve puzzles.

Advantages of PoS Mining:

- **Energy Efficiency:** PoS is far less energy-intensive than PoW, as it does not require solving complex puzzles. This makes it a more sustainable consensus mechanism, particularly for blockchains aiming to reduce their environmental impact.
- **Reduced Entry Barriers:** PoS reduces the need for expensive hardware, making it more accessible to a broader range of participants. All that is required to become a validator is owning and

staking a sufficient amount of the network's cryptocurrency.
- **Incentivized Holding:** By requiring participants to stake coins, PoS incentivizes long-term holding and network loyalty, which can help stabilize cryptocurrency prices.

Disadvantages of PoS Mining:

- **Wealth Concentration:** One of the criticisms of PoS is that it tends to favor those who already hold large amounts of the cryptocurrency. This can lead to wealth concentration, where the richest participants have the most control over the network.
- **Security Concerns:** While PoS is generally secure, it is vulnerable to different attack vectors than PoW, such as long-range attacks or the nothing-at-stake problem. However, many PoS networks have implemented countermeasures to address these concerns.

Profitability in PoS Mining:

Profitability in PoS mining is primarily influenced by the amount of cryptocurrency staked, the reward structure of the network, and the overall performance of the coin. Validators typically earn rewards in proportion to their stake, but their profits also depend on the market value of the staked coins.

III. Various Mining Algorithms and Investment Opportunities

Cryptocurrency mining is a crucial aspect of blockchain ecosystems, ensuring the validation of transactions and the security of decentralized networks. At the core of the mining process are cryptographic algorithms, which define how miners solve complex puzzles to validate blocks and earn rewards. These algorithms play a vital role in determining the efficiency, profitability, and accessibility of mining, as well as the broader health of the blockchain ecosystem. Some of the most prominent mining algorithms include Scrypt,

Equihash, and RandomX, each with its distinct features and implications for miners and investors.

1. Major Mining Algorithms

The choice of mining algorithm can significantly influence the mining experience, ranging from the hardware required to the profitability potential and environmental impact. Three of the most widely used algorithms are Scrypt, Equihash, and RandomX. They have been adopted by major cryptocurrencies, each catering to different use cases and mining approaches.

Scrypt

Scrypt is a proof-of-work (PoW) mining algorithm initially introduced by Colin Percival in 2009 as part of the Tarsnap online backup service. However, it became widely known after its adoption by Litecoin, a popular cryptocurrency that aimed to provide faster and more accessible mining than Bitcoin. Scrypt was designed to be a more memory-intensive algorithm than Bitcoin's SHA-256, reducing the likelihood of large mining farms dominating the network.

Key Features:

- **Memory-Intensive:** Unlike SHA-256, Scrypt requires significant memory (RAM) to perform mining operations. This makes it harder to develop Application-Specific Integrated Circuits (ASICs) for Scrypt, at least in the early stages of its use, as large memory requirements increase hardware complexity and cost.
- **Accessibility for GPU and CPU Mining:** In its early years, Scrypt was friendly to GPU and even CPU miners, as its memory requirements made it difficult for ASIC miners to dominate. This created a more decentralized mining landscape compared to Bitcoin.
- **Faster Block Generation:** Scrypt was designed to enable faster block generation times compared to Bitcoin. For example, Litecoin has a block time of 2.5 minutes, much faster than Bitcoin's 10 minutes, allowing for quicker transaction confirmation and a more fluid network.

Mining with Scrypt:

Initially, Scrypt was considered an ASIC-resistant algorithm, meaning that miners using GPUs or CPUs could compete effectively. However, over time, ASIC miners specifically designed for Scrypt emerged, gradually making GPU and CPU mining less profitable for large-scale miners. Nevertheless, Scrypt remains popular for smaller altcoins, allowing individual miners to participate without the significant investment required for more hardware-intensive algorithms.

Cryptocurrencies Using Scrypt:

- **Litecoin:** The most well-known cryptocurrency using Scrypt, Litecoin was developed as a faster and more accessible alternative to Bitcoin.
- **Dogecoin:** Originally a meme coin, Dogecoin has gained popularity for its active community and frequent use for tipping online. It also uses Scrypt, making it accessible for miners who want to mine alongside Litecoin (through merged mining).

Equihash

Equihash is another PoW mining algorithm, developed by Alex Biryukov and Dmitry Khovratovich in 2016. It is an asymmetric memory-hard algorithm designed to be efficient for verification but memory-intensive for miners. Equihash is best known for its use in privacy-focused cryptocurrencies such as Zcash.

Key Features:

- **ASIC-Resistant:** Equihash was specifically designed to resist ASIC miners by requiring significant memory, similar to Scrypt. The goal was to ensure that mining remained accessible to GPU miners, reducing the centralization risks associated with ASIC dominance.
- **Memory-Intensive and Parallelism:** Equihash relies on high memory usage, requiring miners to have access to substantial RAM. This parallelism benefits GPU mining, where multiple processes can be run simultaneously, making it more difficult for ASICs to gain a competitive edge.

- **Privacy Features:** Equihash is often associated with privacy coins, especially Zcash. Zcash's use of zero-knowledge proofs (zk-SNARKs) for private transactions has made Equihash a popular choice for blockchain projects prioritizing privacy and anonymity.

Mining with Equihash

Equihash mining favors GPUs because of the algorithm's memory requirements and parallel processing capabilities. It was designed to be ASIC-resistant, although, as with Scrypt, ASIC miners have eventually been developed for Equihash, albeit with limited market penetration. Nonetheless, Equihash remains one of the more GPU-friendly algorithms, encouraging decentralized mining across diverse hardware configurations.

Cryptocurrencies Using Equihash:

- **Zcash:** Zcash is the leading cryptocurrency utilizing Equihash. It emphasizes privacy, allowing

users to shield transaction details using zero-knowledge proofs.
- **Horizen (ZEN):** Horizen is another cryptocurrency that uses Equihash, focusing on privacy and scalable blockchain solutions for enterprise use.

RandomX

RandomX is a PoW algorithm designed specifically for CPU mining, launched in 2019 by the Monero project. The algorithm was created in response to the increasing centralization of mining power through the use of ASICs. RandomX attempts to level the playing field by making CPU mining more competitive and discouraging the development of ASIC miners.

Key Features:

- **CPU-Focused:** RandomX was designed to prioritize CPU mining, making it less efficient for GPUs and almost impossible for ASIC miners. This encourages decentralization, as anyone with a standard desktop or server CPU can participate in mining.

- **Random Code Execution:** RandomX works by running random code and using memory-heavy techniques, which makes it difficult to optimize the algorithm for specialized hardware. This means that CPUs are well-suited for RandomX mining without the need for expensive hardware.
- **Privacy and Decentralization:** Like Equihash, RandomX has found its niche in privacy coins, especially Monero. Its CPU-friendly nature ensures that mining can be performed by a wide range of participants, contributing to the decentralization of the network.

Mining with RandomX:

RandomX offers opportunities for miners who may not have access to expensive hardware like ASICs or high-performance GPUs. By enabling CPU mining, RandomX democratizes mining and makes it more accessible to individual miners. However, due to the increasing computational demands of the algorithm, profitability is often lower than with ASIC or GPU mining, depending on the hardware used.

Cryptocurrencies Using RandomX:

- **Monero:** Monero is the most well-known cryptocurrency using RandomX. As a privacy-focused coin, Monero emphasizes decentralization and anonymity, aligning with RandomX's goals of preventing mining centralization through ASICs.

2. The Impact of Algorithms on Mining Profitability and the Ecosystem

The choice of mining algorithm has far-reaching effects on the profitability of mining operations, the sustainability of blockchain networks, and the overall health of the ecosystem. Factors such as hardware accessibility, energy consumption, and network decentralization are heavily influenced by the mining algorithm a blockchain chooses.

Mining Profitability

Mining profitability depends on several factors, including the difficulty of mining (which adjusts based on the total network hashrate), the rewards for successfully mining a block, the cost of electricity, and the efficiency of the mining hardware. Algorithms like Scrypt, Equihash, and RandomX each present unique profitability challenges and opportunities for miners.

Scrypt:

- **Merged Mining Opportunities**: Scrypt miners can take advantage of merged mining, where they mine multiple cryptocurrencies simultaneously. For example, Litecoin and Dogecoin can be mined together, improving profitability without needing additional hardware.
- **Profitability for Small Miners:** As ASICs have entered the Scrypt mining space, profitability for small miners using CPUs and GPUs has decreased. However, altcoins that still use Scrypt may offer niche opportunities for smaller miners.

Equihash:

- GPU-Friendly: Equihash's emphasis on memory-hard computations makes it accessible for GPU miners. This has allowed individual miners and smaller mining pools to remain competitive, especially in privacy-centric cryptocurrencies like Zcash.
- Challenges with ASICs: While initially ASIC-resistant, Equihash has seen some ASIC miners developed specifically for it. This has impacted profitability for GPU miners, though the algorithm remains more decentralized than SHA-256-based mining.

RandomX:

- CPU-Based Profitability: RandomX is one of the few algorithms that favors CPU mining, providing opportunities for miners with standard hardware. Although the rewards are often lower due to Monero's smaller market cap compared to Bitcoin

or Ethereum, the lower barrier to entry makes it attractive for small-scale miners.
- Energy Efficiency: Compared to ASIC-driven algorithms, RandomX is more energy-efficient, helping miners lower operational costs.

Network Decentralization and Ecosystem Health

The mining algorithm chosen by a blockchain has a direct impact on the network's decentralization and overall ecosystem health. Algorithms that favor ASICs often lead to the centralization of mining power in the hands of a few large-scale operations. In contrast, algorithms that prioritize accessibility for CPU and GPU miners help maintain decentralization by allowing a broader range of participants.

Scrypt:

- Initially Decentralized, Later Centralized: Scrypt started as an ASIC-resistant algorithm, promoting decentralization through accessible GPU mining. However, as ASICs were developed for Scrypt,

mining power began to centralize, especially in major cryptocurrencies like Litecoin.
- Decentralization Through Merged Mining: One redeeming feature of Scrypt is its support for merged mining, which can distribute mining rewards across multiple networks, encouraging broader participation.

Equihash:

- Focus on Decentralization: Equihash was designed to resist ASICs and promote GPU mining, contributing to a more decentralized network. However, the emergence of ASICs for Equihash has slightly undermined this goal, though privacy-focused coins like Zcash continue to prioritize decentralized mining.

RandomX:

- Strong Decentralization: RandomX's focus on CPU mining ensures that a wide range of participants can contribute to Monero's network, promoting decentralization. This is crucial for privacy-focused networks, where centralization could undermine the anonymity and security of users.

3. Investment Opportunities in Mining

Mining presents several investment opportunities, from hardware investments in ASICs or GPUs to participation in mining pools or cloud mining services.

Hardware Investment

Investing in mining hardware is one of the most direct ways to enter the cryptocurrency mining space. However, the type of hardware needed depends on the algorithm in use.

- **ASICs for Scrypt:** High-performance ASICs are essential for profitable mining in Scrypt-based networks like Litecoin. However, the high upfront cost and energy consumption mean that only large-scale operations can make substantial profits.

- **GPUs for Equihash:** While ASICs have been developed for Equihash, GPU mining is still viable, especially for smaller privacy coins. Investing in GPUs offers more flexibility, as they can be used to mine multiple cryptocurrencies.
- **CPUs for RandomX:** RandomX presents a unique opportunity for miners with limited resources. Investing in high-performance CPUs allows entry into Monero mining without the need for specialized hardware.

Cloud Mining and Mining Pools

For those unwilling or unable to invest in hardware, cloud mining services and mining pools offer alternative avenues for profiting from mining.

- **Cloud Mining:** Cloud mining allows investors to lease mining power from large operations. This removes the need for physical hardware but often comes with risks, such as untrustworthy providers or fluctuating profitability.

- **Mining Pools:** Joining a mining pool is a popular strategy for miners who want to earn consistent rewards. By combining computational power, miners in a pool can find blocks more frequently, leading to more stable returns.

Cryptocurrency Investments

Instead of directly engaging in mining, some investors opt to invest in cryptocurrencies that use specific algorithms. For example, investors may choose to hold Monero due to its focus on decentralization through RandomX or invest in privacy coins like Zcash, which uses Equihash. These investments allow exposure to the mining ecosystem without the need to actively mine.

Chapter 3: Cryptocurrency Investment Strategies

I. Understanding the Basics of Trading

The world of cryptocurrency trading offers diverse opportunities for investors, with spot trading and futures trading being two of the most prevalent forms. Each carries its own unique set of implications, benefits, and risks. In addition, successful navigation of these markets requires robust risk management practices and the ability to analyze market data effectively. This section will break down the fundamentals of spot and futures trading, explain how they work, and highlight their impact on investors. Furthermore, it will provide insights into managing risk in volatile markets through comprehensive data analysis.

1. Spot Trading and Futures Trading

Spot trading and futures trading are the two core types of trades that investors to engage in the buying and selling of assets. While both deal with the movement of assets, they operate on different timelines and strategies, which significantly influence how they are used and the types of risks they carry.

Spot Trading

Spot trading refers to the purchase or sale of an asset (in this case, cryptocurrencies) at its current market price. In spot trading, transactions happen "on the spot," with both the buyer and seller agreeing to exchange the asset immediately. The assets are typically delivered and settled quickly, often within one to two days. The price at which these trades occur is called the spot price, reflecting the real-time value of the asset.

In the context of cryptocurrency, spot trading takes place on centralized exchanges like Binance or Coinbase or decentralized exchanges like Uniswap. Investors can trade a variety of digital assets, ranging from Bitcoin and Ethereum to lesser-known altcoins. Spot trading is generally favored by those looking to own and hold the asset for an extended period, waiting for its price to appreciate before selling it. This strategy is often referred to as "HODLing" (a misspelling of "hold" that has become a meme in the cryptocurrency world).

Advantages of Spot Trading:

- **Ownership of Assets:** In spot trading, investors own the actual asset (cryptocurrency) once the transaction is complete, making it a straightforward approach for long-term investors.
- **Simplicity:** Spot trading is simpler to understand than futures trading, especially for beginners, since there are no complicated mechanisms such as contracts or expirations.
- **Liquidity:** Cryptocurrency spot markets are often highly liquid, especially for major assets like Bitcoin, allowing for easy entry and exit from trades.

Disadvantages of Spot Trading:

- **Exposure to Volatility:** The cryptocurrency market is notorious for its volatility. While this can result in significant gains, it also exposes investors to substantial losses.
- **Limited Leverage:** Spot trading generally does not offer the leverage available in futures trading. This means investors cannot amplify their positions to the same extent, potentially limiting profit potential.

Futures Trading

Futures trading, by contrast, involves contracts that agree to buy or sell an asset at a predetermined price on a future date. In futures trading the asset itself (e.g., cryptocurrency) is not traded directly; instead, traders speculate on the asset's price movements by buying or selling contracts based on their predictions of where the price will go.

In a typical cryptocurrency futures trade, an investor might enter a contract to buy Bitcoin at a set price in three months. If Bitcoin's price rises above the contracted price, the trader can profit by fulfilling the contract at the agreed price and selling it at the current (higher) market price. Conversely, if the price drops, the trader faces a loss. Futures contracts allow traders to profit from both rising and falling markets by going long (buying contracts) or short (selling contracts).

Advantages of Futures Trading:

- **Leverage:** Futures trading offers leverage, meaning traders can control larger positions than their initial investment. For example, with 10x leverage, an investor can control $10,000 worth of Bitcoin with only $1,000. This leverage can lead to outsized gains on small price movements.
- **Hedging Opportunities:** Futures contracts are often used to hedge against price volatility. For instance, a Bitcoin miner can lock in a price for their mined Bitcoin through a futures contract,

protecting against potential drops in the asset's price.
- **Speculation on Both Sides:** Futures trading allows traders to profit from price movements in both directions—going long in bullish markets and short in bearish markets.

Disadvantages of Futures Trading:

- **High Risk of Leverage:** While leverage can magnify profits, it also amplifies losses. A small movement in the wrong direction can result in significant losses, even liquidation of the initial capital if the margin is insufficient.
- **Complexity:** Futures trading is more complex than spot trading and often requires a deeper understanding of market dynamics, leverage, margin requirements, and contract expirations.
- **No Ownership of Assets:** In futures trading, traders do not actually own the underlying asset. Instead, they are speculating on its price

movements, which might not appeal to long-term investors interested in asset ownership.

2. Risk Management and Market Analysis

Cryptocurrency markets are inherently volatile, making effective risk management crucial for traders, whether engaging in spot or futures trading. Without a robust risk management strategy, investors can experience significant losses, especially in a market characterized by sharp and unpredictable price swings. Additionally, using data analysis to evaluate market trends can provide critical insights, helping traders make informed decisions.

Risk Management in Volatile Markets

Managing risk in cryptocurrency markets requires a balanced approach to minimize losses while maximizing potential gains. Below are key strategies for risk management:

1. Position Sizing

Position sizing involves determining the right amount of capital to allocate to a single trade. In a highly volatile market, risking too much capital on a single trade can lead to significant losses. Traders often use the 1-2% rule, meaning they only risk 1-2% of their capital on any given trade. For instance, if a trader has $10,000 in their portfolio, they should not risk more than $100-$200 on a single trade. This strategy ensures that no single loss has a devastating impact on the overall portfolio.

2. Setting Stop-Loss Orders

Stop-loss orders are pre-set instructions that automatically close a trade when the asset's price reaches a specified level. This mechanism is essential in futures trading, where leverage can rapidly erode an investor's capital if the market moves against them. For example, if an investor buys Bitcoin futures at $50,000 and sets a stop-loss at $48,000, the position will automatically close if the price falls to $48,000, preventing further losses. Similarly, take-profit orders can lock in gains when an asset's price hits a certain target.

3. Diversification

Diversifying a portfolio across different assets reduces the impact of poor performance in any single asset. In cryptocurrency trading, this could mean holding a mix of established coins like Bitcoin and Ethereum along with smaller, emerging altcoins. While diversification cannot eliminate risk, it can reduce the portfolio's exposure to market volatility by spreading it across various assets with different risk profiles.

4. Leverage Control

In futures trading, it's tempting to use high leverage to amplify profits, but this also significantly increases risk. Traders need to carefully control leverage and avoid over-leveraging positions. Using smaller amounts of leverage, such as 2x or 3x instead of 10x or 20x, can help reduce risk while still providing some upside potential.

Market Analysis

Data analysis is at the heart of managing risk in cryptocurrency trading. Volatility in the market makes it crucial for traders to constantly monitor and analyze data to inform their decisions. The two primary types of market analysis are technical analysis and fundamental analysis.

1. Technical Analysis

Technical analysis involves studying price charts and using historical price data to predict future price movements. Common technical indicators include:

- **Moving Average Convergence Divergence (MACD):** MACD is used to identify changes in a trend's strength, direction, momentum, and duration. When the MACD line crosses above the signal line, it's a bullish signal; when it crosses below, it's a bearish signal.
- **Relative Strength Index (RSI):** RSI measures the speed and change of price movements, indicating whether an asset is overbought or oversold. An RSI

above 70 suggests the asset is overbought, while an RSI below 30 indicates it is oversold, helping traders make buy or sell decisions.

2. Fundamental Analysis

Fundamental analysis focuses on evaluating the intrinsic value of an asset based on external factors, such as the development team behind a cryptocurrency, its use cases, market demand, and overall adoption trends. For instance, a cryptocurrency with strong technological innovations and a solid user base is likely to appreciate in value over time. Understanding the fundamentals of a cryptocurrency can provide long-term insights into its potential, allowing traders to make more informed decisions.

II. Trading Strategies and Technical Analysis

In the fast-moving and highly volatile world of cryptocurrency trading, a strong grasp of technical analysis and a well-crafted trading strategy are key to achieving profitability. Technical analysis helps traders identify patterns in price movements and predict future trends, while specific strategies can enhance the odds of capitalizing on market opportunities. Two of the most widely used technical indicators in cryptocurrency trading are the Moving Average Convergence Divergence (MACD) and the Relative Strength Index (RSI). Understanding how to use these indicators, combined with effective strategies for maximizing profits, can significantly improve a trader's performance in both short-term and long-term trades.

1. Technical Analysis and Key Indicators

Technical analysis involves examining historical price and volume data to forecast future price movements in a cryptocurrency. The underlying assumption is that all market fundamentals, including supply and demand, are reflected in the asset's price. While many tools and indicators are available, MACD and RSI are two essential indicators that offer insights into momentum and trend strength.

1. *Moving Average Convergence Divergence (MACD)*

The Moving Average Convergence Divergence (MACD) is a trend-following momentum indicator that shows the relationship between two moving averages of a cryptocurrency's price. It is designed to reveal changes in the strength, direction, momentum, and duration of a trend. The MACD consists of three main components:

- **MACD Line:** This is calculated by subtracting the 26-period exponential moving average (EMA) from the 12-period EMA.
- **Signal Line:** A 9-period EMA of the MACD line that serves as a trigger for buy and sell signals.
- **Histogram:** A graphical representation showing the difference between the MACD line and the signal line. When the MACD line crosses above the signal line, the histogram turns positive, and when

the MACD line crosses below the signal line, the histogram turns negative.

How to Use MACD in Cryptocurrency Trading:

- **Crossover Signals:** The most common trading signal from the MACD is the crossover between the MACD line and the signal line. When the MACD line crosses above the signal line, it is a bullish signal indicating a potential buying opportunity. Conversely, when the MACD line crosses below the signal line, it is a bearish signal that suggests selling.
- **Identifying Momentum:** The MACD histogram can also be used to gauge momentum. As the histogram grows larger in positive territory, it indicates increasing bullish momentum, and as it grows larger in negative territory, it signals strengthening bearish momentum.
- **Divergence:** Another important feature of the MACD is divergence. When the price of a cryptocurrency moves in the opposite direction of

the MACD, it signals a potential reversal. For instance, if prices are making higher highs while the MACD is making lower highs, it suggests that bullish momentum is weakening, and a bearish reversal may be imminent.

Practical Example:

Imagine a scenario where Bitcoin has been in a steady uptrend for several weeks. A trader who uses the MACD indicator might observe that the MACD line crosses above the signal line, signaling a continued upward momentum. At this point, the trader may enter a long position, expecting prices to keep rising. However, if the trader sees a bearish divergence where Bitcoin's price continues to rise while the MACD starts to flatten or turn downward, they might consider exiting the trade to avoid being caught in a potential downturn.

2. Relative Strength Index (RSI)

The Relative Strength Index (RSI) is a momentum oscillator that measures the speed and change of price movements. It is calculated by comparing the magnitude of recent gains to recent losses to determine whether a cryptocurrency is overbought or oversold. RSI ranges from 0 to 100, with three key levels:

- **70 and above:** Indicates that an asset is overbought and could be due for a price correction.
- **30 and below:** Suggests that an asset is oversold and may be poised for a price rebound.
- **50:** A neutral level that represents a balance between buying and selling pressure.

How to Use RSI in Cryptocurrency Trading:

- **Overbought and Oversold Conditions:** Traders use the RSI to identify overbought or oversold conditions. When the RSI crosses above 70, it may signal that the cryptocurrency is overbought, and traders might consider selling or taking profits.

Conversely, when the RSI drops below 30, it suggests the asset is oversold, providing a potential buying opportunity.

- **Divergence:** Like the MACD, RSI divergence can signal potential trend reversals. If the price makes a new high while the RSI does not, it indicates weakening momentum, and a reversal could occur.
- **Centerline Crossover:** The 50-level on the RSI acts as a dividing line between bullish and bearish momentum. When the RSI crosses above 50, it suggests that buyers are gaining control, while a drop below 50 indicates that sellers are dominating.

Practical Example:

Suppose Ethereum has experienced a sharp rally, and its RSI has climbed above 70. A trader could interpret this as an overbought condition and may prepare to take profits or exit the trade. Conversely, if Ethereum's RSI dips below 30 after a prolonged decline, it could indicate an oversold market, signaling a buying opportunity for traders who anticipate a price recovery.

2. Strategies for Maximizing Profits

With a solid understanding of key indicators like MACD and RSI, traders can develop effective strategies to maximize profits in the cryptocurrency market. The following are some widely used trading strategies that leverage technical analysis to enhance profitability.

1. Trend Following Strategy

A trend-following strategy is one of the simplest and most popular strategies in cryptocurrency trading. The basic principle is to buy when the price is trending upwards and sell when it is trending downwards. This strategy works well in strong trending markets where prices move in a consistent direction.

How to Execute a Trend Following Strategy:

- **Identify the Trend:** Use indicators such as moving averages or MACD to identify whether the market is in an uptrend or downtrend.

- **Entry and Exit:** Enter a trade when the indicators confirm the trend direction. For instance, if the MACD line crosses above the signal line, it could be a signal to enter a long trade in a bullish market. Exit the trade when the trend shows signs of reversal, such as a bearish MACD crossover or an RSI above 70 indicating overbought conditions.
- **Position Sizing:** In a trend-following strategy, position sizing is crucial. Start with smaller positions and add to them as the trend strengthens.

Advantages:

- Works well in trending markets.
- Easy to implement for beginners.

Disadvantages:

- Can result in losses during range-bound markets.
- Late entry and exit points might reduce profitability.

2. Mean Reversion Strategy

The mean reversion strategy is based on the idea that the price of a cryptocurrency will eventually return to its average or "mean" after deviating from it. This strategy is useful in range-bound or sideways markets where prices oscillate between support and resistance levels.

How to Execute a Mean Reversion Strategy:

- **Identify Overbought/Oversold Conditions:** Use RSI or Bollinger Bands to identify when the price has deviated significantly from its average. If RSI is above 70, indicating overbought conditions, prepare for a potential price correction. If RSI is below 30, signaling oversold conditions, look for a price rebound.
- **Entry and Exit:** Enter a trade when the price starts to revert toward its mean after being overbought or oversold. For example, in an oversold condition, buy the asset as the RSI starts to move back above 30.

Exit the trade when the price approaches its mean or key resistance level.

Advantages:

- Effective in sideways or range-bound markets.
- Offers multiple trading opportunities in choppy markets.

Disadvantages:

- Can be risky in strong trending markets where price deviations continue for extended periods.
- Requires precise timing for entry and exit.

3. Breakout Strategy

A breakout strategy aims to capture large price movements that occur after the price breaks through key support or resistance levels. This strategy works well in volatile markets, where sudden price shifts can create significant profit opportunities.

How to Execute a Breakout Strategy:

- **Identify Key Levels:** Use support and resistance levels or trendlines to identify areas where the price has consistently bounced off. The more times the price has tested these levels, the more significant the breakout is likely to be.

- **Confirmation of Breakout**: Confirm the breakout with indicators like MACD or RSI. A bullish breakout might occur when the price crosses above resistance, and the RSI moves above 50, signaling increasing buying momentum.

- **Entry and Exit:** Enter the trade when the price breaks through the resistance level (in an upward breakout) or support level (in a downward breakout). Set a stop-loss just below the breakout level to protect against false breakouts. Exit the trade when the price shows signs of consolidation or reversal.

Advantages:

- Captures large price movements in volatile markets.

- High profit potential if the breakout leads to a strong trend.

Disadvantages:

- High risk of false breakouts.
- Requires quick decision-making and proper risk management.

4. Scalping Strategy

Scalping is a short-term strategy focused on making small, frequent profits by taking advantage of minor price fluctuations throughout the day. Scalpers aim to enter and exit trades quickly, often within minutes, and accumulate profits over time.

How to Execute a Scalping Strategy:

- **Identify Small Price Movements:** Use short time frames (e.g., 1-minute or 5-minute charts) and technical indicators like MACD and RSI to identify short-term price fluctuations.

- **Entry and Exit:** Enter a trade when the indicators show a small price movement in your favor, and exit quickly before the price reverses. For example, if the RSI moves above 50 on a 1-minute chart, it may signal a brief upward movement, allowing the trader to enter a quick long trade.
- **High Volume Trading:** Scalping requires high trade volume to accumulate profits, as each individual trade yields small gains.

Advantages:

- Provides many trading opportunities throughout the day.
- Limits exposure to long-term market risks.

Disadvantages:

- Requires constant monitoring and quick execution.
- High transaction costs can eat into profits.

III. Comparison of Long-term and Short-term Investment Strategies

Cryptocurrency investment strategies can generally be categorized into two main approaches: short-term trading and long-term holding. Each strategy has its distinct characteristics, risks, and rewards. Understanding these differences is crucial for investors looking to navigate the volatile and rapidly changing cryptocurrency market effectively. In this section, we will explore the nuances of short-term investment profits and long-term cryptocurrency holding strategies, including the well-known concept of HODLing.

1. Short-term Investment Profits

Understanding Short-term Trading

Short-term trading, often referred to as day trading or swing trading, involves buying and selling cryptocurrencies within a short time frame—ranging from minutes to weeks. Traders utilizing this strategy aim to capitalize on price fluctuations and market volatility to generate profits quickly.

1. Risks of Short-term Trading

- **Market Volatility:** The cryptocurrency market is notorious for its extreme volatility. Prices can swing dramatically within short periods, presenting both opportunities and risks for short-term traders. While significant price movements can lead to substantial profits, they can also result in considerable losses if trades are not executed wisely.
- **Emotional Decision-making:** Short-term trading often involves high pressure and fast decision-making, which can lead to emotional trading. Traders may react impulsively to market fluctuations, leading to poor decisions based on fear or greed rather than sound analysis.
- **Transaction Costs:** Frequent trading incurs transaction fees, which can eat into profits. Traders must be aware of the impact of these

costs, particularly when attempting to capitalize on small price movements.

- **Time Commitment:** Successful short-term trading requires constant monitoring of the markets and technical analysis. It can be time-consuming and demanding, especially for those with other professional or personal commitments.

2. Rewards of Short-term Trading

- **Quick Profits:** The primary advantage of short-term trading is the potential for rapid profits. Traders can take advantage of short-lived market trends and price movements to generate significant returns in a relatively short period.
- **Liquidity:** Short-term trading often benefits from high liquidity in the cryptocurrency market, allowing traders to enter and exit positions quickly without significantly impacting prices.
- **Flexibility:** Short-term traders can adapt to changing market conditions, allowing them to

switch strategies or focus on different assets based on current trends. This flexibility can be advantageous in a rapidly evolving market.

- **Learning Experience:** Engaging in short-term trading can enhance traders' understanding of the market dynamics, technical analysis, and risk management. The experience gained can be beneficial for developing long-term investment strategies.

Short-term trading can be lucrative for those willing to invest time and effort into understanding the market. However, it comes with significant risks and requires discipline, strategy, and the ability to manage emotions. Investors considering short-term trading should approach it with caution and be prepared for the possibility of losses.

2. Long-term Cryptocurrency Holding Strategies

Understanding Long-term Holding

Long-term investment strategies, often referred to as "HODLing" (a misspelling of "holding" that has become a meme in the cryptocurrency community), involve buying cryptocurrencies and holding onto them for an extended period—often years—regardless of market fluctuations. This approach is grounded in the belief that cryptocurrencies will appreciate in value over time, providing significant returns.

1. Benefits of Long-term Investments

- **Less Stressful:** Long-term investors are not typically concerned with short-term price fluctuations. This approach can lead to less stress and emotional turmoil, as investors can ride out market volatility without feeling the need to react immediately.
- **Potential for Higher Returns:** Historical data suggests that many cryptocurrencies have experienced significant appreciation over longer

periods. Long-term investors may benefit from substantial capital gains as the market matures and adoption increases.

- **Simplicity and Ease:** Long-term holding requires less active management than short-term trading. Investors can purchase assets and monitor them periodically rather than constantly analyzing market conditions and executing trades.
- **Tax Advantages:** In many jurisdictions, long-term capital gains are taxed at a lower rate than short-term gains. This tax efficiency can enhance overall returns for long-term investors.
- **Alignment with Market Trends:** Many long-term investors believe that the broader trend of increasing cryptocurrency adoption and integration into mainstream finance will lead to sustained growth over time. This belief can provide confidence in holding assets despite short-term price fluctuations.

2. Risks of Long-term Holding

- **Market Volatility:** While long-term investors can ride out short-term volatility, they are still exposed to the overall market risk. A significant downturn in the cryptocurrency market can lead to substantial losses, particularly if the asset does not recover.
- **Opportunity Cost:** Holding assets for the long term means that investors may miss out on short-term trading opportunities that could provide immediate profits. This potential for lost opportunities can be a drawback for some investors.
- **Technological Risks:** The cryptocurrency market is continually evolving, and long-term investors must be aware of technological changes, regulatory developments, and market trends that could impact their investments. Projects may fail, or new technologies may emerge that render existing assets less valuable.

- **Liquidity Risks:** Some cryptocurrencies may not have sufficient liquidity, making it difficult to sell large holdings without impacting the price. Long-term investors should be mindful of the liquidity of their chosen assets.

Long-term holding strategies can be effective for those who believe in the potential of cryptocurrencies and are willing to weather short-term market volatility. This approach allows investors to benefit from the growth of the market over time while minimizing the stress associated with constant trading.

3. Comparing Short-term and Long-term Strategies

1. Time Horizon

The most obvious difference between short-term and long-term strategies is the time horizon. Short-term traders focus on quick profits, while long-term investors aim to benefit from sustained growth over extended periods. This distinction impacts trading behavior, market analysis, and overall investment philosophy.

2. Risk Tolerance

Short-term trading typically involves higher risk due to market volatility and the potential for emotional decision-making. In contrast, long-term holding strategies tend to be less risky in terms of daily price fluctuations but still expose investors to market risks over time. An investor's risk tolerance will influence their choice of strategy.

3. Investment Goals

Investors must consider their financial goals when choosing a strategy. Short-term traders may aim for quick gains, while long-term investors often seek to build wealth over time. Understanding one's investment objectives is crucial for determining the appropriate approach.

4. Market Conditions

Market conditions can also influence the effectiveness of each strategy. In highly volatile markets, short-term trading may provide opportunities for profit, while stable or bullish markets may favor long-term holding. Investors should adapt their strategies based on prevailing market trends.

5. Skills and Knowledge

Short-term trading requires a deep understanding of technical analysis, market trends, and trading strategies. It often demands constant learning and adaptation. Long-term investors may benefit more from a broader understanding of fundamental analysis and market trends, focusing on projects with strong long-term potential.

4. The Concept of HODLing

HODLing Philosophy

The HODLing philosophy is grounded in the belief that cryptocurrencies, particularly Bitcoin, will continue to appreciate in value as adoption grows. HODLers typically resist the urge to sell during market downturns, believing that long-term value will ultimately prevail. This mindset is especially popular among investors who view cryptocurrencies as a hedge against traditional financial systems and inflation.

Benefits of HODLing

- **Simplicity:** HODLing is straightforward; investors purchase assets and hold them without the need for frequent trading.
- **Psychological Resilience:** HODLers learn to resist the fear of missing out (FOMO) and panic selling, leading to a more disciplined investment approach.

- **Long-term Capital Gains:** HODLing can be tax-efficient, as long-term capital gains are often taxed at lower rates than short-term gains.

HODLing Risks

- **Market Risks:** HODLers remain exposed to market risks, and a prolonged bear market can result in significant losses.
- **Technological Risks:** Projects may fail or become obsolete, impacting the value of HODLed assets.
- **Opportunity Cost:** HODLing may lead to missed opportunities in the short-term trading space.

Chapter 4: Growth and Prospects of the Cryptocurrency Market

I. **Global Mining Market and Cryptocurrency Growth Rates**

The global cryptocurrency mining market has experienced exponential growth in the past decade, driven by the increasing demand for decentralized currencies like Bitcoin and Ethereum. However, the practices and regulatory frameworks surrounding cryptocurrency mining vary significantly across different countries, influenced by factors such as energy availability, political climate, and technological infrastructure. Understanding these regional differences is crucial for both investors and miners, as local regulations and practices can drastically affect profitability, sustainability, and growth prospects.

In this section, we will explore the global mining market by analyzing mining environments in various countries, followed by a statistical analysis of the cryptocurrency market's growth trajectory. This includes trends in mining profitability, market capitalization, and the impact of innovation and regulation on the growth rates of digital currencies.

1. Mining Environments by Country

Cryptocurrency mining practices differ significantly based on geography, largely due to the availability of cheap energy, supportive policies, and local technological advancements. Below is an overview of the key mining environments around the world:

1. China

Historically, China was the dominant player in cryptocurrency mining, accounting for as much as 65-75% of the global Bitcoin mining hash rate until mid-2021. This dominance was driven by China's abundance of cheap coal-based and hydroelectric energy in regions like Sichuan, Inner Mongolia, and Xinjiang. Despite its initial stronghold on mining, China's government cracked down on cryptocurrency activities in 2021, including mining, due to concerns over financial risks, environmental impact, and capital flight.

As a result, many mining farms were forced to either shut down or relocate to more mining-friendly nations. The regulatory shift caused a significant drop in China's mining market share, but some miners have gone underground, continuing operations under the radar.

- **Impact on the market:** China's regulatory crackdown led to a global redistribution of the Bitcoin hash rate. Miners began seeking more favorable environments, contributing to the diversification of the global mining market. However, China's position as a technological powerhouse means that it could still play a role in mining innovation, especially in areas like hardware production and blockchain research.

2. United States

The United States emerged as a key player in the global mining market following China's crackdown. Several states with cheap, renewable energy sources—such as Texas, Washington, and New York—have become mining hubs due to their abundant access to hydroelectric power and wind energy. Texas, in particular, has attracted miners with its deregulated energy market and favorable regulatory environment. The state is known for its low energy costs, pro-business policies, and growing infrastructure for mining operations.

In addition to energy advantages, the U.S. benefits from a robust technological ecosystem, which includes access to mining hardware and expertise. Companies in the U.S. have also been more proactive in adopting greener energy solutions, aligning their operations with environmental, social, and governance (ESG) principles to attract investors concerned about sustainability.

- **Impact on the market:** The U.S. has become a global leader in cryptocurrency mining, contributing significantly to the global hash rate. Regulatory clarity, compared to other countries, has also made the U.S. an attractive environment for large-scale mining operations, including publicly listed mining companies. The focus on renewable energy solutions in states like Texas positions the U.S. as a pioneer in sustainable mining practices.

3. Russia

Russia is another major player in the global cryptocurrency mining market. The country offers favorable conditions for mining due to its cold climate and surplus of cheap energy, particularly from natural gas and hydroelectric sources. The Siberian region, with its low temperatures and proximity to energy reserves, is a popular destination for mining farms.

Despite these advantages, Russia's regulatory stance on cryptocurrency has been inconsistent. While mining is not illegal, the country's central bank has expressed concerns about the potential risks associated with cryptocurrencies, including financial stability and illicit activities. As of 2024, Russia is still in the process of developing a clear regulatory framework for cryptocurrency mining, which creates uncertainty for miners operating in the region.

- **Impact on the market:** Russia's energy surplus and cold climate make it an ideal location for mining, but the lack of regulatory clarity has limited its potential to become a global leader in the market. Miners in Russia must navigate a complex and sometimes hostile regulatory environment, which can hinder growth.

4. Kazakhstan

Kazakhstan has rapidly emerged as a key player in the global cryptocurrency mining scene, particularly after China's crackdown. The country's abundant coal resources and relatively lax regulatory environment have attracted numerous mining companies looking for cheap energy. Kazakhstan's government has been supportive of mining, viewing it as a way to bolster its economy through increased energy consumption and tax revenue.

However, Kazakhstan's mining boom has also led to significant challenges, particularly related to energy consumption. Mining farms have been blamed for widespread power shortages in the country, leading the government to introduce energy tariffs for miners and explore renewable energy options to mitigate the strain on the national grid.

- **Impact on the market:** Kazakhstan's rise in the global mining market has been rapid, but its reliance on coal-based energy raises concerns about environmental sustainability. The introduction of tariffs and potential regulatory changes could affect the country's attractiveness as a mining hub in the future.

5. Canada

Canada has positioned itself as a leader in sustainable cryptocurrency mining, thanks to its abundant access to renewable energy sources, particularly hydroelectric power. Provinces like Quebec and British Columbia have become popular destinations for mining operations due to their low energy costs and favorable climate, which reduces cooling expenses for mining rigs.

Canada's regulatory environment is generally supportive of blockchain and cryptocurrency innovation, making it an attractive destination for mining companies. The country also benefits from a strong technological infrastructure and a skilled workforce, which contribute to the growth of its mining industry.

- **Impact on the market:** Canada's focus on sustainability and renewable energy makes it a model for eco-friendly mining practices. The country's regulatory stability and access to clean energy have positioned it as a global leader in the cryptocurrency mining market.

6. Iran

Iran has also emerged as a significant player in the global cryptocurrency mining market, largely due to its access to cheap electricity from fossil fuels and hydroelectric power. The government has supported mining as a way to generate revenue, particularly in light of economic sanctions that have limited Iran's access to the global financial system. However, Iran's mining industry is subject to frequent regulatory changes, including temporary bans on mining during periods of high electricity demand.

- **Impact on the market:** While Iran's cheap energy makes it an attractive location for mining, the volatile regulatory environment and the impact of international sanctions create uncertainty for miners operating in the region.

2. Market Growth Rates: A Statistical Analysis of the Cryptocurrency Market

The global cryptocurrency market has experienced remarkable growth since the launch of Bitcoin in 2009. As of 2024, the market is valued at over $1 trillion, with the total market capitalization of cryptocurrencies growing by over 500% in the past five years. Several key factors have contributed to this growth, including increased adoption of cryptocurrencies as investment assets, institutional interest, and the rise of decentralized finance (DeFi) platforms.

1. Bitcoin Mining Hash Rate

The Bitcoin mining hash rate, a measure of the total computational power used in the Bitcoin network, has grown significantly since 2009. The hash rate is closely tied to market growth, as higher hash rates indicate more competition among miners and greater network security. The global hash rate reached an all-time high in 2023, following the redistribution of mining power after China's crackdown.

2. Market Capitalization

The total market capitalization of all cryptocurrencies surpassed $3 trillion at its peak in 2021, though it has since fluctuated due to market corrections. Bitcoin remains the dominant cryptocurrency, accounting for approximately 45-50% of the total market cap. Ethereum follows as the second-largest cryptocurrency, driven by its smart contract functionality and the growth of DeFi.

3. Energy Consumption and Sustainability

Cryptocurrency mining's environmental impact has been a growing concern, particularly with the energy-intensive nature of Proof of Work (PoW) mining. Studies estimate that Bitcoin mining alone consumes more electricity annually than some small countries. This has led to calls for more sustainable mining practices, particularly through the adoption of renewable energy sources and the transition to Proof of Stake (PoS) consensus mechanisms, which consume significantly less energy.

4. Institutional Adoption

One of the key drivers of market growth has been the increasing interest from institutional investors. Companies like Tesla, MicroStrategy, and Square have invested billions of dollars in Bitcoin, while major financial institutions like JPMorgan and Goldman Sachs have begun offering cryptocurrency-related products and services to their clients.

5. Regulatory Developments

Regulatory clarity has played a critical role in shaping market growth. Countries with clear regulatory frameworks, like the U.S. and Canada, have attracted significant investment in both mining and trading. On the other hand, regions with unclear or hostile regulatory environments, like China and India, have seen slower growth or market exits.

II. Eco-friendly Mining and Energy Consumption Issues

As cryptocurrency has risen in popularity, so have concerns about its environmental impact. One of the key criticisms of cryptocurrency mining, particularly for Proof of Work (PoW) currencies like Bitcoin, is the energy-intensive nature of the process. Cryptocurrency mining requires powerful computers to solve complex mathematical problems, consuming large amounts of electricity. This energy consumption has led to widespread debate about the sustainability of the practice, especially as global energy needs continue to rise and concerns about climate change become more pressing.

In response, the industry has begun exploring eco-friendly mining practices and technological innovations to address these concerns. From utilizing renewable energy to developing new consensus mechanisms, these efforts are transforming cryptocurrency mining and addressing its energy consumption issues. This section will explore examples of eco-friendly mining practices and examine the technological approaches that are being implemented to solve the industry's energy problems.

- **Examples of Eco-Friendly Mining**

The adoption of renewable energy sources is one of the most promising approaches to making cryptocurrency mining more sustainable. The transition from fossil fuels to renewables like solar, wind, and hydroelectric power can significantly reduce the environmental footprint of mining operations. Below are examples of how renewable energy is transforming cryptocurrency mining across different regions.

1. Hydroelectric Power in Canada and Iceland

Two of the most well-known examples of eco-friendly mining operations are in Canada and Iceland. Both countries have abundant access to hydroelectric power, which is one of the cleanest and most reliable sources of renewable energy.

In Canada, provinces like Quebec and British Columbia have become popular locations for cryptocurrency mining operations due to their access to cheap, renewable hydroelectric power. The cold climate also helps reduce cooling costs for mining rigs, further increasing the efficiency of mining operations. Quebec, in particular, has attracted mining companies from around the world, drawn by the region's low electricity costs and stable regulatory environment.

Iceland offers a similar advantage. The country is known for its abundant renewable energy resources, particularly hydroelectric and geothermal power. The cold climate also helps keep mining equipment from overheating, minimizing the need for additional energy for cooling. Iceland's combination of renewable energy and natural cooling makes it an ideal location for eco-friendly cryptocurrency mining operations. In fact, nearly 100% of Iceland's electricity comes from renewable sources, making it one of the greenest mining locations in the world.

Impact on the market: Both Canada and Iceland demonstrate how access to renewable energy can make cryptocurrency mining more sustainable. By utilizing hydroelectric and geothermal power, mining companies in these regions are significantly reducing their carbon footprints, setting an example for other countries to follow. These regions are becoming models for sustainable mining practices, attracting environmentally conscious investors and companies.

2. Solar Mining in Texas

The U.S. state of Texas has emerged as a major hub for cryptocurrency mining, thanks to its deregulated energy market and abundant renewable energy resources, particularly solar power. Texas receives some of the highest levels of solar radiation in the country, making it an ideal location for solar energy projects. As more mining companies move to the state, they are increasingly turning to solar power to fuel their operations.

Several mining companies in Texas have built or are in the process of building solar-powered mining farms. These operations use large solar farms to generate electricity, powering mining rigs without relying on fossil fuels. By using solar energy, these companies can significantly reduce their environmental impact and contribute to the growth of renewable energy infrastructure in the state.

In addition to solar power, Texas is also a leader in wind energy. Many mining operations in the state are powered by a combination of solar and wind energy, further reducing their reliance on fossil fuels.

Impact on the market: Texas is quickly becoming a global leader in renewable energy-powered cryptocurrency mining. The state's growing renewable energy infrastructure, combined with its favorable regulatory environment, makes it an attractive destination for mining companies looking to minimize their environmental impact. Solar and wind-powered mining operations in Texas are not only reducing their carbon footprints but also helping to drive innovation in renewable energy technology.

3. Wind-powered Mining in Scandinavia

Scandinavia has also become a prominent region for eco-friendly cryptocurrency mining, thanks to its abundant renewable energy resources, particularly wind power. Countries like Norway and Sweden have access to vast amounts of clean energy, making them ideal locations for sustainable mining operations.

In Norway, nearly all of the country's electricity is generated from renewable sources, with hydropower accounting for the majority. However, wind power is becoming an increasingly important part of Norway's energy mix, and several mining companies have begun using wind-powered electricity to fuel their operations.

Sweden is also a leader in renewable energy, particularly wind power. Swedish cryptocurrency mining companies are taking advantage of the country's growing wind energy infrastructure to power their operations. In addition to wind power, Sweden benefits from a cool climate, which helps reduce the need for energy-intensive cooling systems for mining rigs.

Impact on the market: Scandinavia's focus on renewable energy and sustainable practices makes it an ideal region for eco-friendly cryptocurrency mining. Mining companies in Norway and Sweden are leading the way in adopting wind power, setting an example for other countries looking to reduce the environmental impact of cryptocurrency mining. Scandinavia's commitment to sustainability is helping to drive innovation in renewable energy technologies, which could have far-reaching effects on the global mining industry.

4. *Green Mining Initiatives in Kazakhstan*

After China's 2021 crackdown on cryptocurrency mining, Kazakhstan became a major player in the global mining market, attracting many companies due to its cheap energy and favorable regulatory environment. However, Kazakhstan's energy mix is heavily reliant on coal, which has raised concerns about the environmental impact of its mining operations.

In response, several initiatives have been launched to promote green mining in Kazakhstan. These initiatives aim to reduce the reliance on coal and transition to cleaner energy sources, such as wind and solar power. For example, some mining companies in Kazakhstan are investing in renewable energy projects to power their operations, while others are exploring ways to improve energy efficiency and reduce their carbon footprints.

Impact on the market: Kazakhstan's efforts to promote green mining are a positive step toward reducing the environmental impact of cryptocurrency mining in the country. However, the success of these initiatives will depend on the continued development of renewable energy infrastructure and government support for sustainability efforts. If Kazakhstan can successfully transition to cleaner energy sources, it could become a global leader in eco-friendly mining.

- **Technological Approaches to Solving Energy Issues**

Several technological innovations are being developed to reduce the environmental impact of cryptocurrency mining. These innovations aim to make mining more energy-efficient and less reliant on traditional, energy-intensive methods. Below are some of the most promising technological approaches to solving the energy issues associated with cryptocurrency mining.

1. Transition to Proof of Stake (PoS) Consensus Mechanisms

One of the most significant technological developments in the cryptocurrency industry is the transition from Proof of Work (PoW) to Proof of Stake (PoS) consensus mechanisms. PoW, which is used by cryptocurrencies like Bitcoin, requires miners to solve complex mathematical problems to validate transactions and create new blocks. This process is extremely energy-intensive, as it requires a large amount of computational power.

In contrast, PoS consensus mechanisms allow validators to create new blocks and validate transactions based on the number of coins they hold and are willing to "stake" as collateral. Since PoS does not require solving complex mathematical problems, it consumes significantly less energy than PoW.

The most well-known example of a cryptocurrency transitioning to PoS is Ethereum, which completed its long-awaited Ethereum 2.0 upgrade in 2022. This upgrade transitioned the Ethereum network from PoW to PoS, reducing its energy consumption by over 99%.

Impact on the market: The transition to PoS is one of the most effective ways to reduce the environmental impact of cryptocurrency mining. As more cryptocurrencies adopt PoS or similar consensus mechanisms, the overall energy consumption of the industry is expected to decrease. This transition is particularly important for the future sustainability of the cryptocurrency market, as it addresses one of the most significant criticisms of the industry: its energy consumption.

2. Energy-efficient Mining Hardware

Another key area of innovation is the development of energy-efficient mining hardware. Traditional mining rigs, such as ASIC (Application-Specific Integrated Circuit) miners, consume a significant amount of electricity. However, new mining hardware is being designed to be more energy-efficient, allowing miners to achieve the same levels of computational power while using less electricity.

For example, companies like Bitmain and Canaan Creative have developed more energy-efficient ASIC miners that are optimized for cryptocurrency mining. These new-generation mining rigs are capable of performing at higher hash rates while consuming less power, making them more environmentally friendly.

Impact on the market: The development of energy-efficient mining hardware is helping to reduce the overall energy consumption of cryptocurrency mining operations. As more miners adopt these new technologies, the environmental impact of mining is expected to decrease, making the industry more sustainable in the long term.

3. Liquid Cooling Systems for Mining Rigs

Cooling systems are a major source of energy consumption in cryptocurrency mining. Mining rigs generate a large amount of heat during operation, and traditional cooling methods, such as air conditioning, require a significant amount of electricity. To address this issue, some mining companies are turning to liquid cooling systems to improve energy efficiency.

Liquid cooling systems use a liquid coolant to absorb and dissipate heat from mining rigs, reducing the need for energy-intensive cooling methods. These systems are not only more energy-efficient but also help improve the performance and lifespan of mining hardware by preventing overheating.

Impact on the market: The adoption of liquid cooling systems is helping to reduce the energy consumption of mining operations, particularly in regions with warm climates where traditional cooling methods are less effective. By improving the energy efficiency of cooling systems, mining companies can further reduce their environmental impact and lower their overall operational costs.

Chapter 5: Blockchain Regulations and Legal Issues

I. Current Status of Cryptocurrency Regulations in Various Countries

As cryptocurrencies have gained global popularity, they have also attracted the attention of regulators worldwide. Governments are attempting to understand and manage this emerging asset class, balancing innovation with concerns about fraud, money laundering, consumer protection, and market stability. In this section, we will explore the current status of cryptocurrency regulations in three major regions: the United States, Europe, and Asia. We will also examine how these regulations impact cryptocurrency mining and trading, shaping the future of the blockchain ecosystem.

1. U.S., Europe, and Asia: Comparative Analysis of Regulatory Frameworks and Their Effects on Global Markets

The United States

The United States has taken a complex, multi-agency approach to cryptocurrency regulation, with different regulatory bodies overseeing various aspects of the cryptocurrency market. The regulatory environment in the U.S. is often criticized for being fragmented and unclear, leading to uncertainty for businesses and investors alike. However, the U.S. is still home to some of the most significant cryptocurrency exchanges and blockchain technology companies.

- **Securities and Exchange Commission (SEC):** The SEC has been a key player in regulating cryptocurrencies, particularly regarding whether certain digital assets qualify as securities under the Howey Test. If a cryptocurrency is deemed a security, it must comply with the SEC's strict regulatory requirements. For example, the SEC has pursued legal actions against Initial Coin Offerings (ICOs) that have not registered with the agency. The ongoing Ripple case is a landmark trial, as the SEC contends that XRP, Ripple's native token, is a security.

- **Commodity Futures Trading Commission (CFTC):** The CFTC regulates cryptocurrencies that fall under the category of commodities. Bitcoin and Ethereum are classified as commodities, allowing them to be traded on regulated exchanges. The CFTC oversees cryptocurrency derivatives markets and ensures compliance with federal law.

- **Financial Crimes Enforcement Network (FinCEN):** FinCEN primarily focuses on preventing money laundering and the financing of terrorism. It requires cryptocurrency exchanges to adhere to strict anti-money laundering (AML) and know-your-customer (KYC) regulations. Companies must report suspicious activity and ensure that their customers are verified.

- **State-level regulation:** In addition to federal agencies, each state has its own set of regulations governing cryptocurrency businesses. New York's BitLicense, introduced in 2015, is one of the most stringent regulatory frameworks. Companies must obtain a BitLicense to operate in New York, which has led some firms to avoid the state altogether due to the complexity and cost of compliance.

Effects on Global Markets

The U.S. has a profound influence on the global cryptocurrency market, and its regulatory decisions often set precedents that other countries may follow. The uncertainty caused by inconsistent and evolving regulations has led some businesses to relocate to countries with clearer or more favorable regulatory frameworks. However, the U.S. remains a key hub for cryptocurrency development, particularly in terms of innovation, funding, and market liquidity. The increasing involvement of institutional investors and the approval of Bitcoin futures ETFs by the SEC indicate that the U.S. market is slowly becoming more regulated and integrated with traditional financial systems.

Europe

Europe is another major player in the cryptocurrency space, and the regulatory landscape across the continent is beginning to coalesce with a more unified approach through the European Union. However, individual member states have their own regulatory frameworks, leading to some discrepancies in how cryptocurrencies are treated within the EU.

- **European Union's MiCA Regulation:** In 2020, the European Commission proposed the Markets in Crypto-Assets (MiCA) regulation, which aims to create a comprehensive regulatory framework for digital assets across the EU. MiCA will cover areas such as transparency, consumer protection, and the prevention of market abuse. The regulation also seeks to bring cryptocurrency exchanges and wallet providers under its supervision, establishing a common standard for operating in the EU.

- **Anti-Money Laundering (AML) Directive:** The EU has also been proactive in combating money laundering and terrorist financing in the cryptocurrency space. The 5th Anti-Money Laundering Directive (5AMLD) came into force in 2020 and requires cryptocurrency exchanges and wallet providers to implement AML and KYC measures. The upcoming 6th Anti-Money Laundering Directive (6AMLD) is expected to impose even stricter requirements.
- **Country-Specific Regulations:** While MiCA aims to standardize cryptocurrency regulation across the EU, some member states have taken their own regulatory initiatives. For instance, Germany has introduced legislation allowing banks to offer cryptocurrency custody services, while countries like France have implemented their own licensing regimes for cryptocurrency businesses. The United Kingdom, no longer part of the EU, has introduced its own cryptocurrency regulations, overseen by the Financial Conduct Authority (FCA).

Effects on Global Markets

Europe's regulatory approach, particularly with MiCA, is likely to have a significant impact on the global cryptocurrency market. By creating a harmonized framework, the EU is positioning itself as a leader in the regulation of digital assets. Clear and consistent regulations could attract businesses and investors seeking legal certainty, making Europe a major hub for cryptocurrency activity. Additionally, the EU's stance on stablecoins could set global standards for the regulation of digital assets tied to fiat currencies.

Asia

Asia is home to some of the largest cryptocurrency markets in the world, including China, Japan, South Korea, and Singapore. The regulatory environment across Asia is diverse, with some countries embracing cryptocurrencies and others taking a more cautious or even hostile approach.

- **China's Cryptocurrency Ban:** China was once a dominant force in the cryptocurrency mining industry, with over 70% of Bitcoin's hashrate originating from the country. However, in 2021, the Chinese government implemented a comprehensive ban on cryptocurrency mining and trading. The People's Bank of China (PBoC) declared that all cryptocurrency transactions were illegal, citing concerns about financial stability, fraud, and energy consumption. This led to an exodus of miners from China to countries with more favorable regulations, such as the United States, Kazakhstan, and Canada.

- **Japan's Regulatory Framework:** Japan is one of the most cryptocurrency-friendly countries in Asia. The Financial Services Agency (FSA) regulates cryptocurrency exchanges and requires them to be registered. Japan was the first country to officially recognize Bitcoin as legal tender in 2017, and the country has implemented strong consumer protection measures following the Mt. Gox hack. The FSA continues to oversee the market and enforces AML and KYC regulations.

- **South Korea's Approach:** South Korea is another important player in the cryptocurrency space. The country has introduced regulations that require cryptocurrency exchanges to comply with AML and KYC laws, and exchanges must partner with local banks to offer real-name accounts. The government has also introduced taxation on cryptocurrency trading, signaling its intent to regulate the market further. However, South Korea has maintained a cautious stance toward ICOs, effectively banning them.
- **Singapore's Proactive Stance:** Singapore has emerged as a global cryptocurrency hub, thanks to its clear regulatory framework and pro-business environment. The Monetary Authority of Singapore (MAS) regulates cryptocurrency exchanges under the Payment Services Act (PSA), which sets out licensing requirements for various types of digital payment services, including cryptocurrency exchanges. The country has also introduced AML and KYC requirements, but it remains one of the

most welcoming jurisdictions for cryptocurrency businesses.

Effects on Global Markets

Asia's regulatory diversity has created a mixed environment for cryptocurrency markets. China's ban on mining and trading has had a significant impact, leading to a redistribution of mining activity across the globe. However, the emergence of cryptocurrency-friendly jurisdictions like Japan, South Korea, and Singapore ensures that Asia remains a major player in the global cryptocurrency ecosystem. Singapore, in particular, has attracted businesses and investors seeking regulatory clarity, positioning itself as a leading destination for cryptocurrency innovation.

2. Impact of Regulations on Mining and Trading

Cryptocurrency regulations have a profound effect on both mining and trading activities. Regulations shape the legal framework in which businesses operate, influencing everything from energy usage to consumer protection and market access. Below, we examine how different regulatory approaches impact cryptocurrency mining and trading.

Impact of Regulations on Mining

- **Energy Consumption and Environmental Concerns:** One of the key regulatory concerns surrounding cryptocurrency mining is its high energy consumption. Bitcoin mining, in particular, requires vast amounts of electricity, leading to environmental concerns in countries like China. The Chinese government's decision to ban mining was partly driven by the desire to reduce the country's carbon footprint and conserve energy. Similarly, some European countries have raised concerns about the environmental impact of mining, leading to calls for stricter regulations on energy usage.

   However, some jurisdictions are adopting more environmentally friendly approaches. For example, countries like Iceland and Norway have become popular destinations for cryptocurrency miners due to their abundant renewable energy resources. As the global focus shifts toward sustainability, it is likely that mining operations will increasingly migrate to regions with access to clean energy.

- **Regulation of Mining Equipment and Operations:** In addition to concerns about energy consumption, some governments have introduced regulations targeting the equipment used in cryptocurrency mining. For instance, in some countries, import restrictions have been placed on mining hardware, while others have introduced licensing requirements for mining operations. These regulations can significantly affect the profitability and viability of mining in certain regions.
- **Taxation of Mining Profits:** Mining profits are subject to taxation in many jurisdictions. In countries like the United States, cryptocurrency miners are required to report their earnings as income, and they may also be subject to capital

gains tax when they sell their mined coins. Tax policies can impact the attractiveness of mining as a business activity, influencing where miners choose to operate.

Impact of Regulations on Trading

- **Exchange Licensing and Compliance:** One of the most significant regulatory challenges for cryptocurrency exchanges is compliance with local laws. In regions like the United States and Europe, exchanges must obtain licenses to operate, and they are subject to strict AML and KYC requirements. These regulations ensure that exchanges are operating legally and transparently, protecting consumers from fraud and market manipulation. However, they can also create barriers to entry for new exchanges, limiting competition in some markets.
- **Taxation of Cryptocurrency Trading:** Taxation policies also have a significant impact on cryptocurrency trading. Many countries treat

cryptocurrencies as taxable assets, meaning that traders must report their profits and pay taxes on gains. In countries with high tax rates, this can reduce the attractiveness of trading, leading some investors to seek out jurisdictions with more favorable tax policies.

- **Market Stability and Investor Protection:** Regulatory frameworks that emphasize market stability and investor protection can enhance the legitimacy of cryptocurrency trading. By implementing measures such as investor protection funds and strict disclosure requirements, governments can reduce the risks associated with cryptocurrency investments, encouraging more participation from retail and institutional investors.

II. Legal Issues with Smart Contracts

Smart contracts, one of the most revolutionary applications of blockchain technology, are self-executing contracts with the terms of the agreement directly written into code. These contracts automatically enforce themselves based on predefined conditions, eliminating the need for intermediaries such as lawyers or banks. While smart contracts offer numerous benefits, including transparency, security, and efficiency, they also raise significant legal challenges. In this section, we will explore the legal implications of smart contracts, the challenges they present, and potential institutional solutions to mitigate risks.

1. Challenges and Effectiveness: Legal Implications of Smart Contracts

Smart contracts operate on decentralized blockchain networks, using code to automate transactions and enforce agreements. This automation is designed to reduce human error and prevent fraud, but it also creates a host of legal complexities that traditional contract law struggles to address.

1. Enforceability and Recognition by Law

One of the fundamental questions regarding smart contracts is their enforceability under existing legal frameworks. Traditional contracts are subject to well-established legal principles, such as offer, acceptance, consideration, and the intention to create legal relations. However, smart contracts do not always fit neatly into these categories. Since they are based on code and executed automatically, there is often no room for negotiation, interpretation, or renegotiation after execution.

Legal systems around the world have been slow to adapt to this new form of contract. In many jurisdictions, the legal status of smart contracts remains ambiguous. For example, traditional contracts can be contested in court if one party believes that there was a misunderstanding or misrepresentation, but with smart contracts, the code is the final arbiter. If a mistake is made in the code, the contract will still execute according to the programmed terms, even if those terms do not reflect the true intentions of the parties involved.

Another challenge is that smart contracts often operate across multiple jurisdictions, raising questions about which laws apply and how disputes should be resolved. If a smart contract is executed on a decentralized network that spans different countries, determining the appropriate legal venue for a dispute becomes problematic.

2. *Issues of Consent and Understanding*

Smart contracts rely on code to execute automatically, but this raises concerns about whether all parties fully understand the terms and implications of the agreement. Traditional contracts are often written in natural language, making it easier for non-experts to comprehend their rights and obligations. In contrast, smart contracts are written in programming languages that require a high level of technical expertise to interpret.

This creates a significant legal issue: can a party truly give informed consent to a contract they cannot read or understand? If one party does not fully grasp the code, they may inadvertently agree to terms that are unfavorable or unclear. Courts may be hesitant to enforce contracts in which one party did not have a reasonable opportunity to understand the agreement, even if the contract was executed flawlessly by the code.

In response to these concerns, legal frameworks may need to evolve to require a natural language translation of the smart contract alongside the code. This would ensure that all parties understand the terms, reducing the risk of disputes and misunderstandings.

3. Immutable Nature of Smart Contracts

One of the defining features of blockchain technology is its immutability: once data is recorded on the blockchain, it cannot be altered. While this feature provides security and transparency, it also poses legal challenges when it comes to smart contracts. In traditional contracts, parties can amend the agreement or renegotiate terms as circumstances change. However, smart contracts are difficult, if not impossible, to modify once they have been deployed.

This immutability becomes problematic in cases where one party needs to amend the contract due to unforeseen circumstances, such as a force majeure event (e.g., natural disaster or government intervention) or mutual agreement to change the terms. Since smart contracts execute automatically and cannot be altered, parties are often left without legal recourse if a contract becomes unworkable or unfair after execution.

Some blockchain platforms are developing mechanisms that allow for smart contract upgrades or amendments, but these solutions are still in their infancy. Moreover, such mechanisms may undermine the immutability of blockchain technology, creating a delicate balance between legal flexibility and the integrity of the blockchain.

4. Dispute Resolution

Smart contracts are designed to execute automatically, theoretically eliminating the need for dispute resolution. However, in practice, disputes can still arise from smart contracts, particularly in cases where the contract does not perform as expected or where one-party claims that the code does not reflect the original agreement.

Traditional dispute resolution mechanisms, such as courts or arbitration, are ill-suited to handle smart contracts, as they are based on human interpretation of written agreements. Since smart contracts operate based on code, legal disputes may require the involvement of technical experts who can analyze the code and determine whether it functioned as intended.

Some blockchain platforms are experimenting with decentralized dispute resolution mechanisms, where a panel of peers can vote on the outcome of a dispute. However, these systems are still in their early stages and may lack the legal authority or recognition necessary to enforce decisions in a court of law.

2. Institutional Solutions: Regulatory Solutions to Mitigate Risks Associated with Smart Contracts

Given the legal challenges posed by smart contracts, institutions and regulators are beginning to explore solutions to mitigate risks and ensure that smart contracts can be used effectively and safely. Below are several potential regulatory solutions that could address the legal issues surrounding smart contracts.

1. Legal Recognition and Standardization

One of the first steps in addressing the legal challenges of smart contracts is to provide them with clear legal recognition. Several countries have already begun to take steps in this direction. For example, in the United States, states like Arizona, Nevada, and Tennessee have passed laws recognizing the legal enforceability of smart contracts. These laws typically state that a contract cannot be denied legal effect or enforceability solely because it is executed via blockchain technology.

However, a more unified approach is needed at the national and international levels. Standardizing the legal treatment of smart contracts across jurisdictions would provide businesses and individuals with greater confidence in using them. Governments could work together to develop global guidelines for smart contracts, addressing issues such as consent, enforceability, and dispute resolution.

2. Code Audits and Certification

One way to mitigate the risks associated with poorly written or misunderstood smart contracts is to introduce third-party code audits or certification. Just as traditional contracts are often reviewed by lawyers, smart contracts could be reviewed by independent technical experts who verify that the code accurately reflects the intended agreement.

Certification could become a legal requirement for certain types of smart contracts, particularly those used in high-stakes industries such as finance, insurance, or real estate. By ensuring that smart contracts are properly coded and secure, regulators could reduce the risk of disputes and improve the overall reliability of blockchain-based contracts.

3. *Natural Language Translations*

To address the issue of consent and understanding, regulators could require that all smart contracts include a natural language version of the agreement alongside the code. This would ensure that all parties can fully understand the terms of the contract before agreeing to it.

Incorporating natural language translations into smart contracts would also make it easier for courts or arbitrators to resolve disputes, as they would not need to rely solely on technical analysis of the code. Instead, they could refer to the natural language version to interpret the parties' intentions and resolve conflicts.

4. Amendment Mechanisms

As discussed earlier, the immutability of smart contracts can create legal challenges when parties need to amend or update the agreement. One solution is to develop standardized mechanisms for upgrading or amending smart contracts, allowing parties to modify the contract under certain conditions.

These mechanisms could be governed by strict rules to prevent abuse. For example, any amendments could require the consent of all parties involved, and the blockchain could record the amendment process to ensure transparency and accountability. Additionally, regulators could set guidelines for when amendments are permissible, such as in cases of force majeure or mutual agreement.

5. Decentralized Dispute Resolution

Given the global and decentralized nature of blockchain technology, traditional courts may not be the most effective venue for resolving disputes related to smart contracts. Instead, decentralized dispute resolution mechanisms could be developed to provide a more efficient and cost-effective way of handling conflicts.

Platforms such as Kleros are experimenting with decentralized arbitration systems, where disputes are resolved by a panel of peers who analyze the smart contract and vote on the outcome. While these systems are still in their early stages, they offer a promising alternative to traditional dispute resolution methods. Regulators could work to formalize and standardize these systems, ensuring that they provide fair and legally binding outcomes.

6. Consumer Protection Mechanisms

Regulators may need to introduce consumer protection mechanisms to address the risks associated with smart contracts. This could include requiring disclosures about the risks of smart contracts, implementing cooling-off periods during which parties can back out of a contract, and providing legal remedies for individuals who enter into smart contracts without fully understanding the terms.

Consumer protection measures could also extend to businesses that use smart contracts, ensuring that they are not exposed to undue risks or liabilities. For example, regulators could require businesses to carry insurance that covers losses resulting from faulty smart contracts or hacking.

III. Regulatory Directions for Investor Protection

As cryptocurrencies and blockchain technology have surged in popularity, the need for robust investor protection mechanisms has become a pressing concern. The decentralized nature of these digital assets, coupled with a largely unregulated market, has exposed investors to various risks, including fraud, hacking, price manipulation, and the collapse of platforms and exchanges. Given the increasing participation of both retail and institutional investors in the cryptocurrency space, governments and regulatory bodies are grappling with how best to safeguard investors while fostering innovation and market growth.

This essay explores the regulatory directions for investor protection in the cryptocurrency market, outlining specific mechanisms that could be implemented to address the unique challenges posed by this rapidly evolving industry. We will delve into key investor protection measures, from transparency requirements and fraud prevention to dispute resolution and the role of regulatory oversight in ensuring a fair and secure market.

1. The Need for Investor Protection in an Unregulated Market

Cryptocurrencies and blockchain technology present a double-edged sword for investors. On the one hand, they offer exciting opportunities for high returns, portfolio diversification, and exposure to cutting-edge financial innovations. On the other hand, they expose investors to a wide range of risks not typically encountered in traditional financial markets. These risks include the volatility of digital assets, the opacity of many blockchain projects, the prevalence of scams, and the vulnerability of cryptocurrency exchanges to cyberattacks.

One of the most significant challenges is that cryptocurrencies and related products often operate in a legal gray area. In many countries, digital assets are not classified as securities, which means they are not subject to the same regulatory standards as traditional financial instruments. This lack of oversight has created an environment ripe for fraud and abuse, with little recourse for investors who fall victim to unscrupulous actors.

Investor protection mechanisms are essential for mitigating these risks and ensuring that the market operates with a high level of integrity. These protections are not only crucial for safeguarding individual investors but also for building trust in the cryptocurrency ecosystem as a whole. Without appropriate regulations, the market will struggle to attract mainstream participants, limiting its potential for growth and long-term sustainability.

2. Investor Protection Mechanisms: Guidelines for Protecting Investors in an Unregulated Market

1. *Transparency and Disclosure Requirements*

One of the most critical investor protection mechanisms in any financial market is the requirement for transparency and disclosure. In traditional markets, companies issuing securities are required to provide detailed information about their financial health, business operations, and potential risks, enabling investors to make informed decisions. A similar framework is needed for cryptocurrencies and blockchain projects to reduce information asymmetry and improve market integrity.

Regulators could mandate that cryptocurrency projects provide clear and comprehensive disclosures about their technology, business model, development team, and potential risks. For example, initial coin offerings (ICOs) or other token sales should be required to present a whitepaper that explains the project's objectives, the functionality of the token, and the legal and regulatory status of the offering. These documents should also include financial projections and risk assessments to give investors a complete picture of what they are buying into.

2. *Anti-Fraud Mechanisms*

Fraud is one of the most significant threats to investor protection in the cryptocurrency space. Ponzi schemes, phishing attacks, and fraudulent ICOs have proliferated in the largely unregulated market, leading to billions of dollars in losses. To combat this, regulators must implement stringent anti-fraud measures that can identify and shut down fraudulent schemes before they harm investors.

One possible solution is to create a centralized registry of legitimate cryptocurrency projects and exchanges. This registry would be maintained by a regulatory body, which would conduct due diligence on each project to ensure that it meets minimum standards of transparency, security, and legal compliance. Investors could consult this registry to verify the legitimacy of a project before investing, reducing their exposure to scams.

Regulatory authorities could also establish more aggressive monitoring and enforcement mechanisms to detect and prosecute fraudulent activities. For instance, blockchain technology itself can be leveraged to track transactions and identify suspicious patterns of behavior. By using machine learning and other advanced data analytics tools, regulators can spot potential fraud in real time and take swift action to prevent further damage.

3. *Investor Education and Awareness Programs*

Another critical component of investor protection is education. Many retail investors who enter the cryptocurrency market lack a deep understanding of how digital assets work, making them particularly vulnerable to fraud, scams, and market manipulation. To address this, regulators and industry groups must prioritize investor education and awareness programs that equip individuals with the knowledge and tools they need to navigate the market safely.

These programs should cover essential topics such as the basics of blockchain technology, the risks and rewards of investing in cryptocurrencies, how to spot fraudulent schemes, and best practices for securing digital assets. Investors should also be educated about the legal and regulatory environment surrounding cryptocurrencies, including their rights and responsibilities as market participants.

Investor education can be delivered through a variety of channels, including online courses, webinars, informational websites, and public service campaigns. Additionally, cryptocurrency exchanges and wallet providers can offer educational resources directly on their platforms, making it easier for users to access critical information before making investment decisions.

4. Security Standards for Cryptocurrency Exchanges

Cryptocurrency exchanges play a central role in the digital asset ecosystem, serving as the primary platforms for buying, selling, and trading cryptocurrencies. However, they are also frequent targets of hacking attacks, with several high-profile breaches resulting in significant losses for investors. Ensuring that exchanges adhere to high-security standards is therefore crucial for investor protection.

Regulatory bodies should establish minimum security requirements for cryptocurrency exchanges, including the use of advanced encryption protocols, two-factor authentication (2FA), cold storage for digital assets, and regular security audits. Exchanges should also be required to maintain sufficient reserves to compensate users in the event of a hack or security breach.

5. Insurance and Compensation Schemes

To further protect investors from losses due to fraud, hacking, or platform failure, regulators could introduce insurance and compensation schemes for cryptocurrency investments. For example, exchanges could be required to purchase insurance policies that cover losses resulting from cyberattacks or other security breaches. These policies would provide investors with financial compensation in the event that their digital assets are stolen or lost.

Such compensation schemes would not only provide a safety net for investors but also help build trust in the cryptocurrency market by demonstrating that governments and industry participants are committed to protecting consumers.

6. Dispute Resolution Mechanisms

Dispute resolution is another critical aspect of investor protection in the cryptocurrency market. Given the decentralized nature of blockchain technology, traditional legal remedies are often difficult to apply to disputes involving digital assets. For instance, if a smart contract executes incorrectly or a transaction is reversed due to a blockchain fork, investors may have little recourse under existing laws.

To address this, regulators could introduce specialized dispute resolution mechanisms tailored to the unique characteristics of blockchain and cryptocurrencies. For example, arbitration or mediation platforms could be developed specifically for resolving disputes related to digital assets. These platforms would allow investors to resolve conflicts quickly and cost-effectively without resorting to lengthy and expensive court proceedings.

7. Regulatory Oversight and Market Surveillance

Finally, regulatory oversight and market surveillance are essential for protecting investors from market manipulation and ensuring that the cryptocurrency market operates fairly and transparently. In traditional financial markets, regulators such as the U.S. Securities and Exchange Commission (SEC) and the Financial Conduct Authority (FCA) in the UK are responsible for monitoring market activity, detecting manipulation, and enforcing rules designed to maintain market integrity.

Similar oversight is needed in the cryptocurrency market to prevent practices such as wash trading, spoofing, and front-running, all of which can distort prices and harm investors. Regulators should work closely with cryptocurrency exchanges to monitor trading activity and ensure compliance with anti-manipulation rules. This could involve using advanced data analytics tools to detect suspicious patterns and identify potential market abuses.

Regulatory bodies could also require exchanges to implement surveillance systems that monitor for illegal or unethical trading practices in real time. These systems would help ensure that market participants adhere to fair trading practices and that investors are not unfairly disadvantaged by manipulative behavior.

Chapter 6: Data Analysis for Cryptocurrency Investment

I. **Methods of Data Analysis in the Cryptocurrency Market**

Data analysis has become an essential component of cryptocurrency investment strategies, providing insights that help investors navigate the often unpredictable and volatile nature of digital asset markets. With thousands of cryptocurrencies actively traded on global exchanges, data-driven analysis can help investors predict market movements, evaluate the performance of individual assets, and make informed decisions about buying, holding, or selling assets.

This section explores the role of data analysis in volatile markets and examines key metrics, including price, trading volume, and hash rate, that investors and analysts can use to gain a deeper understanding of market dynamics.

1. Role of Data in Volatile Markets

Volatility is one of the defining characteristics of cryptocurrency markets. Unlike traditional financial markets, where price movements tend to be relatively stable and predictable, cryptocurrencies often experience rapid and large price swings within short timeframes. This can make investing in digital assets both highly profitable and risky. Data analysis plays a crucial role in mitigating this risk by helping investors identify patterns, predict trends, and make informed decisions based on market behavior.

Predicting Market Movements

In volatile markets, predicting market movements is crucial for investors who want to minimize losses and capitalize on potential gains. Data analysis provides tools for understanding past trends and applying them to future scenarios. By analyzing historical price data, trading volumes, and various on-chain metrics, analysts can identify signals that indicate the potential direction of the market. Some of the methods used to predict cryptocurrency market movements include:

- **Trend Analysis:** One of the most basic methods of predicting market movements is identifying trends. This involves looking at the historical data of a cryptocurrency's price over time to identify whether it is in an uptrend, downtrend, or consolidation phase. By identifying trends early, investors can position themselves accordingly by buying during uptrends or selling during downtrends.
- **Technical Analysis:** Technical analysis involves using charts, indicators, and statistical tools to identify patterns in price and volume data. This method helps investors make predictions about future price movements by analyzing past behavior. Common technical indicators such as moving averages, Relative Strength Index (RSI), and Moving Average Convergence Divergence (MACD) are used to gauge market sentiment and momentum.
- **Sentiment Analysis:** Cryptocurrency markets are also influenced by social and media sentiment. Data

analysts often monitor social media platforms, news headlines, and other sentiment indicators to gauge how positive or negative the market feels about a particular cryptocurrency. Positive sentiment can drive prices higher, while negative sentiment can cause a sell-off.

- **On-Chain Analysis:** On-chain analysis focuses on blockchain data itself, examining transaction volumes, wallet activity, and the movement of large amounts of funds (known as 'whale movements"). This type of analysis can reveal important trends, such as increased activity on a network, which may signal upcoming price movements or market shifts.
- **Quantitative Models:** Advanced quantitative models, including machine learning algorithms, are also employed to predict market behavior. These models take large datasets and apply predictive analytics techniques to forecast future market movements. Machine learning algorithms are trained to identify patterns that may not be

immediately apparent to human analysts, improving the accuracy of predictions.

Managing Risk Through Data

In a volatile market, risk management is just as important as predicting market movements. Data analysis provides the tools needed to identify risks and adjust investment strategies accordingly. By analyzing volatility data, analysts can determine how much risk is associated with a particular cryptocurrency and whether it aligns with the investor's risk tolerance. Additionally, data can be used to create stop-loss levels, which trigger automatic sales if a cryptocurrency's price falls below a certain threshold, helping to limit losses in case of unexpected market downturns.

2. Key Metrics That Drive Market Movements

Cryptocurrency markets are influenced by a variety of data points and metrics, each of which provides valuable insights into market behavior. While there are many different metrics that investors can analyze, three of the most important and widely used are price, trading volume, and hash rate. Each of these metrics plays a crucial role in shaping market sentiment and influencing investment decisions.

1. Price

Price is the most visible and frequently analyzed metric in any financial market, and the cryptocurrency market is no different. The price of a cryptocurrency reflects its current value on the open market and is influenced by a variety of factors, including supply and demand dynamics, market sentiment, and broader macroeconomic trends.

Price Trends and Movements

The price of a cryptocurrency can fluctuate significantly within short periods, making it an important metric for investors looking to profit from short-term trades or time the market for long-term investments. By analyzing historical price data, investors can identify trends such as:

- **Bullish Trends:** A bullish trend occurs when the price of a cryptocurrency is rising over time. This can indicate positive sentiment in the market, often driven by increased demand, favorable news, or positive developments related to the cryptocurrency (e.g., technology upgrades, partnerships, or regulatory approvals).
- **Bearish Trends:** A bearish trend is characterized by a decline in the price of a cryptocurrency. This can result from negative market sentiment, such as bad news, regulatory crackdowns, or a loss of confidence in the underlying technology or team.

Volatility and Price Movements

Cryptocurrency markets are notorious for their volatility, with price swings of 10% or more within a single day not uncommon. Price volatility can present both opportunities and risks for investors. By analyzing volatility data (often measured using indicators like standard deviation or the Bollinger Bands), investors can identify periods of high or low volatility and adjust their strategies accordingly.

For example, during periods of high volatility, short-term traders may look to capitalize on price swings by buying low and selling high. Conversely, long-term investors may prefer to stay out of the market during volatile periods and instead focus on stable trends.

2. Trading Volume

Trading volume refers to the total number of units of a cryptocurrency that are traded over a specific period (e.g., daily, weekly, or monthly). It is a critical metric because it provides insights into market activity, liquidity, and investor sentiment. Trading volume is often analyzed in conjunction with price movements to determine the strength or weakness of a market trend.

Volume-Price Relationship

The relationship between trading volume and price is essential in understanding market dynamics. In general:

- **High Volume and Price Increase:** When a cryptocurrency's price rises accompanied by high trading volume, it is considered a strong signal of a bullish trend. High trading volume indicates strong interest from buyers, which can drive the price higher.

- **Low Volume and Price Increase:** A price increase with low trading volume may signal a weak or unsustainable rally. This is often a sign of limited buying interest, and the price may retrace soon after the rally.
- **High Volume and Price Decrease:** When a cryptocurrency's price falls with high trading volume, it indicates strong selling pressure. This can signal the beginning of a bearish trend or a market correction.
- **Low Volume and Price Decrease:** A price decrease with low trading volume may suggest that the decline is temporary or lacks conviction from sellers. In this case, the price could stabilize or rebound in the near future.

Liquidity and Market Depth

Trading volume is also closely tied to liquidity, which refers to the ease with which a cryptocurrency can be bought or sold without significantly impacting its price. High trading volume typically indicates a liquid market, where large trades can be executed without causing substantial price fluctuations. Conversely, low trading volume suggests an illiquid market, where large trades can result in significant price changes.

Investors often analyze the order book (a list of buy and sell orders at different price levels) to gauge market depth, which provides additional insights into liquidity. A deep market with many buy and sell orders at various price levels is more liquid and less volatile, while a shallow market may experience significant price swings when large orders are placed.

3. Hash Rate

Hash rate is a unique metric specific to proof-of-work (PoW) cryptocurrencies, such as Bitcoin, Ethereum (before its transition to proof-of-stake), and Litecoin.

Hash rate refers to the total computational power being used to mine and secure a blockchain network. In simple terms, it represents the number of calculations that miners are performing every second to solve the cryptographic puzzles required to validate transactions and add new blocks to the blockchain.

Hash Rate and Network Security

The hash rate is a key indicator of the security and health of a PoW blockchain. A higher hash rate means that more computational power is being devoted to securing the network, making it more resistant to attacks, such as a 51% attack, where a malicious actor could potentially control the network and double-spend coins. Therefore, a rising hash rate is generally seen as a positive sign of network security and miner confidence.

Hash Rate and Price Correlation

There is often a correlation between the hash rate of a cryptocurrency and its price. When the price of a cryptocurrency rises, mining becomes more profitable, incentivizing more miners to join the network, which increases the hash rate. Conversely, when the price falls, mining becomes less profitable, and some miners may stop mining, leading to a decrease in the hash rate.

However, this relationship is not always linear, and other factors, such as changes in mining difficulty, block rewards, and energy costs, can also impact the hash rate. Analyzing the hash rate in conjunction with price movements can provide valuable insights into the health and profitability of a PoW blockchain network.

Mining Difficulty and Profitability

Hash rate is also closely tied to mining difficulty, which adjusts periodically to ensure that blocks are mined at a consistent rate. When the hash rate increases, the network typically increases the difficulty of mining to maintain the target block time (e.g., 10 minutes for Bitcoin). This can affect the profitability of mining, as miners need more computational power to earn the same rewards.

For investors in mining operations, understanding the relationship between hash rate, difficulty, and profitability is crucial for making informed decisions about whether to continue mining or adjust their strategies.

II. Risk Management and Portfolio Optimization

The cryptocurrency market, known for its high volatility and unpredictability, presents both tremendous opportunities and significant risks. For investors looking to navigate this dynamic space, effective risk management and portfolio optimization are essential. Given the diverse array of digital assets available—from Bitcoin to altcoins and emerging tokens—understanding how to mitigate risk and optimize returns is critical for long-term success.

This section focuses on two key components of risk management and portfolio optimization: diversification strategies and the use of advanced statistical tools like Value at Risk (VaR) and Monte Carlo simulations. Both techniques allow investors to better manage their exposure to risk while maximizing potential returns.

1. Diversification Strategies: Best Practices for Managing Risk Through Diversification

Diversification is a foundational principle in traditional finance and equally applicable in the cryptocurrency market. In essence, diversification involves spreading investments across a range of assets to reduce exposure to the risk associated with any single asset. By doing so, investors can reduce the potential downside while still maintaining exposure to high-growth opportunities.

Why Diversification Matters in Cryptocurrency

In cryptocurrency markets, prices can be extremely volatile, often swinging by double-digit percentages within a single day. This volatility can be attributed to several factors, including regulatory uncertainty, technological developments, market sentiment, and broader economic trends. Investing in a single cryptocurrency, no matter how established, exposes investors to heightened risk because price fluctuations can be sudden and severe.

Diversification helps mitigate this risk by spreading investment capital across multiple cryptocurrencies with different risk and return profiles. For example, Bitcoin and Ethereum are relatively more established and stable compared to smaller altcoins, while newer tokens may offer higher growth potential but come with more significant risks.

Benefits of Diversification

- **Reduced Risk:** Diversification reduces the risk of significant losses. If one asset in the portfolio underperforms, the gains from other assets can offset those losses. In the cryptocurrency market, this is particularly important, given the frequent price fluctuations of individual coins.
- **Exposure to Various Opportunities:** By diversifying, investors can gain exposure to different sectors of the cryptocurrency ecosystem,

such as decentralized finance (DeFi), privacy coins, stablecoins, and layer-2 scaling solutions. This allows investors to benefit from growth in multiple areas of the industry.

- **Enhanced Long-Term Growth:** A well-diversified portfolio has the potential for enhanced long-term growth. While some assets in the portfolio may experience temporary downturns, others may continue to grow, balancing the overall performance.

Types of Diversification

There are several approaches to diversification in the cryptocurrency market, each offering distinct advantages based on an investor's risk tolerance, goals, and market outlook.

1. *Diversification by Cryptocurrency Market Capitalization*

One of the simplest ways to diversify is by market capitalization. Large-cap cryptocurrencies, like Bitcoin and Ethereum, are considered more stable, while mid-cap and small-cap altcoins offer higher growth potential but carry more risk. A balanced portfolio might include a mix of large-cap assets for stability and smaller-cap assets for potential higher returns.

- **Large-cap cryptocurrencies:** These include well-established cryptocurrencies like Bitcoin (BTC), Ethereum (ETH), and Binance Coin (BNB). They generally have lower volatility and are more widely accepted by institutions and investors, making them a safer bet for long-term stability.
- **Mid-cap and small-cap cryptocurrencies:** These include lesser-known or newer projects that may not have achieved mass adoption but have significant growth potential. Examples include coins like Chainlink (LINK), Polkadot (DOT), and more speculative altcoins.

2. Diversification by Cryptocurrency Sector

The cryptocurrency ecosystem is diverse, with different sectors representing various use cases and technologies. Diversifying across different sectors can help investors capitalize on growth in different areas of the market.

- **DeFi Tokens:** Decentralized Finance (DeFi) projects, such as Aave (AAVE), Uniswap (UNI), and Compound (COMP), are focused on disrupting traditional financial systems by enabling decentralized lending, borrowing, and trading. Investing in DeFi tokens can provide exposure to the growing adoption of decentralized financial services.
- **Privacy Coins:** Coins like Monero (XMR) and Zcash (ZEC) are focused on enhancing privacy and security in cryptocurrency transactions. Privacy coins cater to individuals seeking to protect their financial privacy in an increasingly surveillance-driven digital world.
- **Stablecoins:** Stablecoins like Tether (USDT), USD Coin (USDC), and Dai (DAI) are pegged to fiat currencies like the US dollar, offering stability and liquidity. Stablecoins serve as a hedge against

volatility, allowing investors to park their assets during turbulent market conditions.

- **Layer-2 Solutions and Scalability Projects:** Cryptocurrencies like Polygon (MATIC) and Optimism (OP) offer scaling solutions to improve the efficiency and speed of transactions on major blockchain networks. These projects aim to address the scalability issues that plague networks like Ethereum.

3. Diversification by Geography

Cryptocurrency markets can also be impacted by regional differences, such as regulatory environments, adoption rates, and government policies. Diversifying investments across different geographic regions can help mitigate risks associated with regulatory crackdowns or adoption challenges in a particular country.

For example, some investors may choose to allocate a portion of their portfolio to cryptocurrencies with significant adoption in Asia (e.g., NEO or VeChain) to benefit from the growth of blockchain technology in the region.

4. Diversification by Investment Strategy

Investors can diversify their portfolios by employing different investment strategies. For example, some assets may be held for long-term growth potential (HODLing), while others may be traded actively for short-term profits. By balancing long-term and short-term investments, investors can take advantage of both strategies without overexposing themselves to one.

2. Portfolio Optimization Tools: Using Advanced Statistical Methods to Optimize Investment Portfolios

While diversification is a critical aspect of risk management, portfolio optimization goes one step further by applying advanced statistical methods to enhance portfolio performance. Tools such as Value at Risk (VaR) and Monte Carlo simulations are widely used in traditional finance to measure and optimize the risk-return profile of a portfolio. These tools are increasingly being applied to cryptocurrency investments as well.

Value at Risk (VaR)

Value at Risk (VaR) is a statistical measure used to estimate the potential loss of an investment portfolio over a specified time period, given a certain level of confidence. VaR helps investors understand the potential downside risk of their portfolio and make informed decisions based on their risk tolerance.

How VaR Works

VaR provides a range of possible losses that a portfolio could experience over a given time horizon (e.g., one day, one week, or one month). For example, if a portfolio has a one-day VaR of $10,000 at a 95% confidence level, this means there is a 95% chance that the portfolio will not lose more than $10,000 in a single day.

Applying VaR in Cryptocurrency Portfolios

Given the high volatility of the cryptocurrency market, VaR can be a valuable tool for assessing risk. It can help investors:

- **Set Risk Limits:** By knowing the maximum potential loss in different scenarios, investors can set risk limits and adjust their portfolios accordingly to stay within their desired risk parameters.
- **Compare Risk Across Assets:** VaR allows investors to compare the risk of different cryptocurrencies or portfolios, helping them make decisions about which assets to include or exclude from their investments.

Limitations of VaR

While VaR is a useful risk management tool, it is not without limitations. One of the main criticisms of VaR is that it does not account for extreme market events or "black swan" scenarios, where losses may exceed expectations. For this reason, VaR is often used in conjunction with other risk management tools.

Monte Carlo Simulations

Monte Carlo simulations are a statistical technique used to model and simulate the potential outcomes of an investment portfolio under different scenarios. This tool is particularly valuable in volatile markets, as it allows investors to assess a wide range of possible outcomes based on different market conditions.

How Monte Carlo Simulations Work

Monte Carlo simulations involve running thousands (or even millions) of random simulations based on different variables, such as asset prices, volatility, and correlation between assets. The goal is to generate a distribution of possible portfolio outcomes, helping investors understand the range of potential returns and risks.

Advantages of Monte Carlo Simulations in Cryptocurrency

- **Scenario Analysis:** Monte Carlo simulations allow investors to explore how their portfolio might perform under various market scenarios, such as bull markets, bear markets, or periods of high volatility. This can help investors prepare for different market conditions and make more informed decisions about asset allocation.
- **Risk Assessment:** By simulating thousands of potential market scenarios, investors can assess the probability of different outcomes and identify the level of risk they are willing to take on. For example, an investor may use a Monte Carlo simulation to determine how often their portfolio is likely to experience significant losses or gains.
- **Portfolio Optimization:** Monte Carlo simulations can be used to optimize portfolio allocation by analyzing how different combinations of assets perform across multiple scenarios. This helps

investors identify the optimal mix of assets to maximize returns while minimizing risk.

Limitations of Monte Carlo Simulations

Monte Carlo simulations rely on historical data to model future outcomes, which means they may not fully capture unprecedented market events or rapid shifts in the cryptocurrency landscape. Additionally, the results of Monte Carlo simulations are only as accurate as the input assumptions, so inaccurate data or assumptions can lead to flawed results.

Combining Diversification and Portfolio Optimization

Effective risk management and portfolio optimization require a combination of diversification strategies and advanced statistical tools like VaR and Monte Carlo simulations. By diversifying across multiple cryptocurrencies, sectors, and strategies, investors can reduce risk while maintaining exposure to high-growth opportunities. Meanwhile, tools like VaR and Monte

Carlo simulations help investors assess risk, optimize asset allocation, and prepare for different market scenarios.

Chapter 7: Business Applications of Blockchain Technology

I. Blockchain and Business Model Innovation

Blockchain technology has become one of the most transformative forces in recent years, revolutionizing industries by enabling decentralized, secure, and transparent systems. Its potential to reshape traditional business models is immense, as it offers new ways to manage operations, increase efficiency, and unlock value for companies across various sectors. One of the most significant impacts of blockchain is on the platform economy and automation, where decentralized platforms are reshaping how businesses operate and create value. Moreover, tools like the Business Model Canvas can help organizations structure and implement blockchain-based innovations, providing a framework to integrate this groundbreaking technology into their business strategies.

This section explores how blockchain is driving business model innovation through decentralized platform economies and automation and introduces the Business Model Canvas as a tool for structuring blockchain-based business innovations.

1. Decentralized Platform Economy and Automation: How Blockchain is Driving New Business Models

In the traditional platform economy, companies like Uber, Airbnb, and Amazon act as intermediaries between service providers and consumers, taking a cut of the transactions that happen on their platforms. While these companies have created significant value by connecting users in ways that were not possible before, they also centralize control and data. Blockchain technology is disrupting this model by enabling decentralized platforms where transactions and interactions happen directly between users without the need for a central authority. This shift is driving new business models and redefining the relationship between consumers, providers, and intermediaries.

1. The Rise of Decentralized Platforms

Blockchain's core feature—the distributed ledger—removes the need for intermediaries, as it allows for trustless and transparent transactions. This has given rise to decentralized platforms that facilitate peer-to-peer transactions, often through the use of smart contracts. These platforms eliminate the traditional "middleman" and allow for more efficient, cost-effective, and secure exchanges of goods, services, and information.

Examples of Decentralized Platforms:

- **Decentralized Finance (DeFi) platforms:** DeFi platforms like Uniswap and Aave allow users to lend, borrow, and trade cryptocurrencies without the need for a central authority, such as a bank. Users interact directly with the platform's smart contracts, ensuring transparency and removing the need for intermediaries to process the transactions. DeFi has exploded in popularity, reaching billions of dollars in total value locked (TVL) in just a few years.

- **Decentralized marketplaces:** Platforms like OpenBazaar are challenging traditional e-commerce models by allowing users to buy and sell goods directly, without intermediaries like Amazon or eBay. These decentralized marketplaces use blockchain to secure transactions and verify identities, creating trust between buyers and sellers without relying on a central platform.

- **Decentralized social media:** Traditional social media platforms like Facebook and Twitter control user data and monetize it through advertising. Decentralized alternatives like Minds and Steemit are changing this by giving users ownership of their data and allowing them to be compensated for their content directly, often through cryptocurrency.

2. Smart Contracts and Automation

One of the most powerful features of blockchain is the smart contract—a self-executing contract where the terms of the agreement are written directly into code. Smart contracts automatically execute when the conditions are met, without the need for human intervention. This automation reduces friction, minimizes human error, and increases efficiency, leading to innovative new business models.

For example, in the insurance industry, smart contracts can automate claims processing. If a flight is delayed, a smart contract can automatically trigger a payout to the insured without the need for filing a claim or dealing with an insurance agent. This kind of automation reduces costs and speeds up service, creating a more efficient and user-friendly system.

Applications of Automation:

- **Supply Chain Management:** Blockchain enables companies to track goods across the supply chain in real-time. Smart contracts can automate the release of payments at various stages of the supply chain, ensuring that suppliers are paid instantly when goods are delivered. This reduces delays and improves cash flow for businesses.
- **Automated legal agreements:** Legal agreements that rely on blockchain technology and smart contracts can automate contract enforcement. For example, rental agreements can be encoded into a smart contract, which automatically releases funds to the landlord when the renter occupies the property, ensuring timely and fair transactions without the need for legal oversight.

3. Tokenization and New Ownership Models

Tokenization is another blockchain innovation that is driving new business models. It allows physical and digital assets to be represented as tokens on a blockchain, which can then be bought, sold, or traded. Tokenization opens up new forms of ownership and value exchange, allowing businesses to fractionalize assets or create entirely new markets.

For example, real estate companies can tokenize property, allowing investors to buy fractional shares of buildings. This creates new opportunities for investment and makes it easier for people to invest in assets that were previously inaccessible due to high entry costs. Similarly, companies can tokenize intellectual property or digital art, creating new revenue streams for creators.

In the gaming industry, blockchain is enabling the creation of new ownership models through non-fungible tokens (NFTs). Players can own in-game assets, like skins or weapons, which can be sold or traded on blockchain-based marketplaces. This model gives players more control over their in-game investments and creates new ways for developers to monetize their games.

2. Business Model Canvas for Blockchain Innovation: A Tool for Structuring Blockchain-Based Business Innovations

The Business Model Canvas (BMC), developed by Alexander Osterwalder, is a strategic tool used to develop and document business models. It is a visual chart with nine building blocks that describe how a company creates, delivers, and captures value. The BMC is particularly useful for structuring blockchain-based business innovations, as it helps companies understand how blockchain can enhance or disrupt each component of their business model.

Let's explore how the Business Model Canvas can be applied to blockchain innovation.

1. Key Partners

In a blockchain-based business model, key partners may include developers, blockchain platforms, miners, and governance participants. Partnerships are critical, especially in decentralized networks where various stakeholders work together to maintain and develop the system.

For example, a decentralized finance (DeFi) platform might partner with external auditors to ensure the security of its smart contracts or collaborate with liquidity providers to ensure that users have access to trading pairs.

- **Key question:** Who are the essential partners that will support the implementation and operation of the blockchain technology?

2. Key Activities

Key activities for blockchain-based businesses revolve around maintaining decentralized networks, developing and updating smart contracts, and ensuring the security and scalability of the blockchain. Building trust within the ecosystem is also a key activity, as trustless systems depend on participants' confidence in the underlying technology.

- **Key question:** What critical activities must be performed to maintain and develop the blockchain network?

3. Key Resources

In a blockchain model, key resources include the blockchain infrastructure (nodes, miners, etc.), smart contracts, and the platform's native tokens. Intellectual property and technical expertise in blockchain development are also crucial resources.

For instance, a company that provides decentralized identity solutions will rely on its blockchain infrastructure and cryptographic technology to secure user identities and facilitate authentication.

- **Key question:** What resources are necessary to operate a blockchain-based business, and how can they be efficiently managed?

4. Value Proposition

The value proposition of a blockchain-based business often centers around transparency, security, efficiency, and decentralization. By eliminating intermediaries, blockchain can create more cost-effective and secure processes for users. For example, a decentralized lending platform offers users the ability to access loans without needing a bank, reducing costs and increasing access for underserved populations.

- **Key question:** What unique value does the blockchain provide to customers, and how does it solve their problems more effectively than traditional solutions?

5. Customer Relationships

Blockchain-based business models often promote decentralized and trustless relationships. Customer relationships are facilitated through self-executing smart contracts, which automate many processes and reduce the need for direct human interaction. However, maintaining trust within the ecosystem is still critical, especially in decentralized systems where users may not have direct contact with service providers.

For example, decentralized exchanges like Uniswap rely on automated market-making algorithms rather than human brokers, but they must still build trust through secure code, transparent operations, and a strong community.

- **Key question:** How will the business manage customer relationships in a decentralized and automated environment?

6. Channels

Blockchain businesses typically operate through decentralized networks, which allow customers to access services directly through smart contracts or distributed applications (dApps). Online communities, social media, and open-source platforms are key channels for engaging with users and promoting the platform.

For instance, platforms like Ethereum rely heavily on developer communities to build dApps that drive the ecosystem's growth. Engaging with these communities through hackathons, developer grants, and online forums is essential for growth.

- Key question: What are the most effective channels for reaching and engaging customers in a decentralized ecosystem?

7. Customer Segments

Blockchain-based businesses often target tech-savvy early adopters, cryptocurrency enthusiasts, and users looking for alternatives to traditional financial or technological systems. However, as blockchain becomes more mainstream, customer segments will likely expand to include more traditional users who are drawn to the benefits of decentralization, security, and efficiency.

For example, decentralized finance platforms are initially attracting cryptocurrency users but are beginning to broaden their appeal to more traditional investors looking for higher yields and new financial instruments.

- **Key question:** Who are the key customer segments, and how can blockchain technology meet their unique needs?

8. Cost Structure

Blockchain businesses often have lower operational costs than traditional businesses because they eliminate intermediaries. However, there are still significant costs associated with developing and maintaining blockchain networks, ensuring security, and complying with regulatory requirements.

For example, while decentralized exchanges do not have to pay for the physical infrastructure of a traditional exchange, they do incur costs related to smart contract development, audits, and governance.

Key question: What are the primary costs associated with running a blockchain-based business, and how can they be minimized?

9. Revenue Streams

Revenue streams in blockchain businesses can come from transaction fees, token sales, staking, or offering premium services on decentralized platforms. New revenue models, such as tokenization and decentralized ownership, also enable innovative ways to generate income.

For example, platforms like Ethereum generate revenue through gas fees, while DeFi platforms may charge users a percentage of transactions or offer paid services for higher-tier users.

- **Key question:** How will the blockchain business generate revenue, and what are the most sustainable revenue streams?

II. Blockchain and ESG Investment

Blockchain technology has become an increasingly important tool in the world of business and finance, and its potential to contribute to Environmental, Social, and Governance (ESG) investment is gaining attention. ESG investing focuses on evaluating companies based on their adherence to environmental sustainability, social responsibility, and governance principles. With its decentralized and transparent nature, blockchain offers unique opportunities for aligning with ESG goals. By enabling greater transparency, reducing inefficiencies, and fostering accountability, blockchain technology is creating new pathways for responsible investment and sustainable business practices.

This section explores how blockchain is contributing to environmental sustainability and improving social responsibility and governance in the context of ESG investment.

1. Environmental Sustainability: How Blockchain Technology is Aligning with ESG Principles

One of the core components of ESG investing is environmental sustainability. Investors are increasingly seeking opportunities that align with their values, including reducing carbon footprints, supporting renewable energy, and fostering sustainable practices. Blockchain technology, often associated with high energy consumption due to its use of proof-of-work (PoW) consensus mechanisms in networks like Bitcoin, is also driving innovation in green technology and enabling more sustainable practices across industries.

1. *Energy Efficiency and Renewable Energy Tracking*

Blockchain is playing a pivotal role in promoting renewable energy usage and creating more energy-efficient systems. The technology's inherent transparency allows for real-time tracking of energy consumption and the movement of renewable energy credits, making it easier for companies and investors to verify their sustainability claims.

Blockchain-based Renewable Energy Platforms: Several blockchain platforms have been developed to facilitate the trading and verification of renewable energy credits. One notable example is the Energy Web Foundation (EWF), which is building a decentralized platform to accelerate the adoption of renewable energy. EWF's platform allows energy producers to issue renewable energy certificates on the blockchain, which can be tracked, traded, and verified in real-time.

Similarly, the platform Power Ledger enables peer-to-peer trading of renewable energy. By leveraging blockchain, consumers can buy and sell excess renewable energy, reducing waste and encouraging more widespread use of clean energy. The blockchain records all transactions in an immutable ledger, ensuring that the energy traded is genuinely renewable.

These platforms demonstrate how blockchain is aligning with ESG principles by enabling transparent, accountable systems for tracking and trading renewable energy. This not only supports environmental sustainability but also gives investors confidence that their investments are contributing to real-world sustainability efforts.

2. Carbon Emission Tracking and Offset Markets

One of the most significant challenges in addressing climate change is the lack of transparency and accountability in carbon emissions reporting. Many companies fail to accurately report their emissions, and existing carbon offset programs are often plagued by inefficiencies and fraud. Blockchain technology is helping solve this issue by enabling accurate, verifiable tracking of carbon emissions and facilitating carbon offset markets.

Blockchain for Carbon Offsetting: Platforms like Veridium are using blockchain to track carbon emissions and manage carbon credits. Veridium works with corporations to calculate their carbon footprints and create tokenized carbon credits, which can be traded or used to offset emissions. By tokenizing carbon credits on the blockchain, Veridium ensures that credits are authentic, transparent, and easily transferable. This reduces the risk of double counting and fraud, creating more reliable and efficient carbon offset markets.

Similarly, CarbonX is leveraging blockchain to reward individuals and businesses for reducing their carbon footprints. By creating a marketplace for carbon credits, CarbonX incentivizes sustainable behavior while ensuring that emissions reductions are accurately recorded and verified.

Blockchain's role in carbon tracking and offset markets aligns with ESG goals by promoting accountability and transparency in corporate sustainability efforts. Investors can be confident that companies using blockchain to manage their carbon credits are genuinely working to reduce their environmental impact.

3. *Supply Chain Sustainability*

Supply chains often contribute significantly to a company's carbon footprint and environmental impact. Blockchain technology is being used to create more sustainable supply chains by improving transparency, traceability, and accountability. This allows companies to identify inefficiencies, reduce waste, and ensure that suppliers are adhering to sustainable practices.

Blockchain for Supply Chain Transparency: One of the leading blockchain initiatives in this area is IBM's Food Trust, which is using blockchain to create transparent supply chains for food products. By recording every step of the supply chain on a distributed ledger, IBM's platform allows consumers and businesses to trace the journey of food from farm to table. This helps reduce food waste, ensures that products are sourced sustainably, and holds suppliers accountable for their environmental practices.

Another example is Everledger, a blockchain-based platform for tracking the origin and journey of diamonds. Everledger records every stage of the diamond supply chain, from mining to retail, ensuring that the diamonds are sourced ethically and sustainably. This level of transparency helps companies meet their ESG goals by ensuring that their supply chains are free from conflict and environmentally destructive practices.

By enabling more sustainable and transparent supply chains, blockchain technology is directly contributing to environmental sustainability and helping businesses align with ESG principles.

2. Social Responsibility and Governance: The Role of Governance in Blockchain-Based Systems

In addition to environmental sustainability, ESG investing also focuses on social responsibility and governance. These aspects of ESG evaluate how companies interact with their employees, customers, and communities, as well as how they are governed in terms of leadership, ethics, and transparency. Blockchain technology's decentralized and transparent nature offers unique solutions for improving both social responsibility and governance.

1. Social Responsibility in Blockchain Systems

Blockchain is being used to address social issues such as financial inclusion, fair labor practices, and ethical sourcing. Its ability to create immutable records and enable peer-to-peer transactions without intermediaries makes it an ideal tool for promoting social good.

Financial Inclusion and Access: One of the most significant ways blockchain is contributing to social responsibility is by promoting financial inclusion. In many parts of the world, individuals lack access to basic financial services such as banking, credit, and insurance. Blockchain-based systems are providing solutions by enabling peer-to-peer transactions and creating decentralized financial services (DeFi) that do not require traditional intermediaries.

For example, platforms like Celo and BitPesa are using blockchain to provide financial services to underserved populations in developing countries. Celo allows users to send and receive payments using only a mobile phone, while BitPesa facilitates cross-border payments and remittances in Africa. By providing access to financial services, these platforms are helping individuals lift themselves out of poverty and contribute to economic development.

Fair Labor Practices: Blockchain is also being used to ensure fair labor practices by improving transparency in supply chains. For example, the Provenance platform uses blockchain to verify the origins of products and ensure that they are ethically sourced. This includes verifying that workers are paid fairly and that no forced or child labor is used in the production process. By recording these details on an immutable ledger, Provenance ensures that companies can back up their ethical claims with verifiable data.

2. Governance in Blockchain-Based Systems

Governance is a critical component of ESG investing, and blockchain technology offers innovative solutions for improving governance within organizations. Blockchain's decentralized nature makes it particularly suited to promoting transparency, accountability, and ethical decision-making.

Decentralized Governance Models: One of the most significant innovations in blockchain-based governance is the decentralized autonomous organization (DAO). DAOs are organizations that operate on blockchain-based smart contracts, where decisions are made collectively by token holders rather than a central authority. This decentralized governance model promotes transparency and ensures that decisions are made democratically, reducing the risk of corruption or unethical behavior.

For example, the MakerDAO platform allows token holders to participate in the governance of a decentralized stablecoin. Token holders can vote on important decisions such as interest rates and collateral requirements, ensuring that the platform is governed in a transparent and democratic manner. This type of decentralized governance aligns with ESG principles by promoting ethical decision-making and reducing the influence of centralized power structures.

Improving Corporate Governance: Blockchain technology is also being used to improve governance within traditional corporations. By recording corporate actions, voting results, and shareholder information on a distributed ledger, blockchain can increase transparency and accountability in corporate governance.

For example, companies like Broadridge Financial Solutions are using blockchain to improve shareholder voting systems. Broadridge's platform allows shareholders to vote on corporate actions securely and transparently, ensuring that votes are accurately recorded and counted. This reduces the risk of fraud and promotes greater trust in corporate governance.

Similarly, blockchain is being used to track executive compensation and ensure that it aligns with company performance. By recording compensation packages on a transparent and immutable ledger, companies can ensure that executive pay is based on merit rather than favoritism or corruption.

3. The Role of Blockchain in ESG Investment

Blockchain technology's unique characteristics—transparency, decentralization, and immutability—make it a powerful tool for ESG investing. By enabling real-time tracking of environmental data, promoting social responsibility, and improving corporate governance, blockchain is helping companies and investors align with ESG principles.

For investors, blockchain offers new opportunities to invest in companies that are genuinely committed to sustainability and ethical practices. By leveraging blockchain's transparency, investors can verify that companies are meeting their ESG goals and making real progress toward sustainability.

At the same time, blockchain is helping companies improve their ESG performance by creating more efficient and transparent systems for managing environmental, social, and governance issues. From tracking renewable energy credits to improving supply chain transparency, blockchain is transforming the way companies operate and ensuring that they can meet the growing demand for responsible business practices.

As ESG investing continues to grow, blockchain will play an increasingly important role in driving sustainable and ethical business practices. By enabling greater transparency and accountability, blockchain is helping create a more responsible and equitable global economy.

III. Regulatory Response Strategies Using Data Analysis

In the evolving landscape of blockchain technology and cryptocurrency, navigating regulatory environments is crucial for businesses and investors alike. Regulatory frameworks are rapidly developing as governments and regulatory bodies grapple with the implications of blockchain technology. To stay ahead of these changes, companies need robust strategies for anticipating regulatory shifts and ensuring compliance. Data analysis and smart contracts are emerging as key tools for addressing these challenges, offering innovative ways to predict regulatory changes and automate compliance processes.

This section delves into the use of data analysis for predicting regulatory changes and the role of smart contracts in automating regulatory compliance.

1. **Predicting Regulatory Changes: Data Analysis Techniques to Anticipate Changes in Regulations**

Regulatory environments for blockchain and cryptocurrency are dynamic and can shift rapidly based on technological advancements, economic trends, and political pressures. To effectively manage these changes, businesses can leverage data analysis techniques to predict and respond to regulatory shifts. By analyzing historical data, tracking legislative trends, and utilizing predictive modeling, companies can better prepare for potential regulatory developments.

1. Analyzing Historical Data and Legislative Trends

Historical data analysis involves examining past regulatory changes to identify patterns and trends that could indicate future developments. By reviewing historical regulatory decisions, enforcement actions, and legislative proposals, companies can gain insights into the factors driving regulatory changes.

Key Techniques for Historical Data Analysis:

- **Trend Analysis**: Identifying trends in past regulatory actions can provide clues about the direction of future regulations. For example, if there has been an increasing trend in regulations targeting data privacy, it may indicate a growing emphasis on privacy-related laws.
- **Comparative Analysis:** Comparing regulatory approaches across different jurisdictions can highlight common regulatory themes and potential areas of convergence. This can help businesses

anticipate how regulations may evolve globally and adapt their strategies accordingly.

- **Legislative Tracking:** Tracking legislative proposals and regulatory updates is crucial for staying informed about potential changes. Tools and platforms that aggregate and analyze legislative data can help businesses monitor proposed regulations, track their progress, and assess their potential impact.
- **Example:** The use of platforms like Regulatory Tracker allows businesses to follow legislative developments in real-time. By analyzing the content of proposed bills and regulations, companies can identify key areas of concern and adjust their compliance strategies accordingly.

2. Utilizing Predictive Modeling and Machine Learning

Predictive modeling and machine learning techniques offer advanced methods for forecasting regulatory changes. These techniques involve using historical data and algorithms to predict future trends and regulatory outcomes.

- **Predictive Modeling:** Predictive modeling involves creating statistical models that use historical data to forecast future events. In the context of regulatory prediction, businesses can use predictive models to estimate the likelihood of specific regulatory changes based on historical patterns and current trends.
- **Example:** A company might use predictive modeling to assess the probability of new data privacy regulations being enacted based on past legislative activity and current political climate. This can help the company prepare for potential regulatory requirements and develop proactive compliance strategies.
- **Machine Learning:** Machine learning algorithms can analyze large volumes of data to identify patterns and make predictions about future regulatory changes. By training algorithms on historical regulatory data, businesses can gain

insights into potential regulatory scenarios and adjust their strategies accordingly.

- **Example:** Machine learning models can be trained to analyze news articles, legislative documents, and social media discussions to identify emerging regulatory trends. This can help companies anticipate regulatory changes and prepare for potential impacts on their operations.

3. Scenario Planning and Risk Assessment

Scenario planning involves creating multiple hypothetical scenarios based on different regulatory outcomes and assessing their potential impact on the business. By developing a range of scenarios, businesses can prepare for various regulatory developments and create contingency plans.

- **Risk Assessment:** Risk assessment involves evaluating the potential risks associated with different regulatory scenarios. By assessing the likelihood and impact of regulatory changes, businesses can prioritize their compliance efforts and allocate resources more effectively.

- **Example:** A financial institution might develop scenarios for potential changes in anti-money laundering (AML) regulations and assess the impact on its compliance processes. This can help the institution identify potential risks and develop strategies to mitigate them.

2. Smart Contracts for Regulatory Compliance: Automating Compliance Through Smart Contract Technology

Smart contracts are self-executing contracts with the terms of the agreement directly written into code. They run on blockchain networks and automatically enforce and execute the terms of the contract when predefined conditions are met. Smart contracts offer significant potential for automating regulatory compliance, reducing manual processes, and ensuring adherence to regulatory requirements.

1. Automating Compliance Processes

Smart contracts can automate various compliance processes, reducing the need for manual intervention and minimizing the risk of human error. By encoding regulatory requirements into smart contracts, businesses can ensure that their operations comply with relevant regulations in real-time.

Key Compliance Areas for Smart Contracts:

- **KYC (Know Your Customer) and AML (Anti-Money Laundering):** Smart contracts can automate KYC and AML processes by verifying customer identities and monitoring transactions for suspicious activity. By integrating with identity verification services and transaction monitoring systems, smart contracts can ensure that businesses comply with regulatory requirements without manual intervention.
- **Example:** A cryptocurrency exchange might use smart contracts to automatically verify the identity of users and flag suspicious transactions. By

automating these processes, the exchange can ensure compliance with KYC and AML regulations while reducing the risk of fraud.

- **Data Privacy and Protection:** Smart contracts can help businesses comply with data privacy regulations by managing and securing sensitive data. By encoding data protection requirements into smart contracts, businesses can ensure that data is handled in accordance with regulatory standards.
- **Example:** A healthcare provider might use smart contracts to manage patient consent for data sharing and ensure that data is only accessed by authorized parties. This can help the provider comply with data privacy regulations such as GDPR or HIPAA.

2. Ensuring Transparency and Accountability

Smart contracts provide a transparent and immutable record of all transactions and contract executions. This transparency helps ensure accountability and reduces the risk of compliance issues.

- **Transparency:** Blockchain technology provides a transparent ledger of all smart contract activities. This transparency allows businesses and regulators to track and verify compliance with regulatory requirements.
- **Example:** A company using smart contracts for supply chain management can provide regulators with a transparent record of all transactions, ensuring that products are sourced ethically and in compliance with environmental regulations.
- **Accountability:** Smart contracts ensure that all parties involved in a transaction or contract adhere to the agreed-upon terms. By automating the enforcement of contract terms, smart contracts reduce the risk of non-compliance and ensure that businesses meet their regulatory obligations.
- **Example:** A financial institution might use smart contracts to automate compliance with reporting requirements. By automatically generating and

submitting reports based on predefined criteria, the institution can ensure timely and accurate compliance.

3. Integrating with Existing Regulatory Frameworks

While smart contracts offer significant potential for automating compliance, they must be integrated with existing regulatory frameworks to be effective. This involves ensuring that smart contracts align with regulatory requirements and can interact with regulatory authorities when necessary.

- **Regulatory Integration:** Businesses must work with regulators to ensure that smart contracts comply with legal and regulatory standards. This may involve developing standards for smart contract development, conducting audits, and obtaining regulatory approvals.
- **Example:** A company developing smart contracts for financial services might work with regulatory authorities to ensure that the contracts comply with

securities regulations and obtain necessary approvals before deploying them.

- **Smart Contract Audits:** Regular audits of smart contracts are essential to ensure that they function as intended and comply with regulatory requirements. Audits can help identify vulnerabilities, ensure code integrity, and verify compliance with legal standards.
- **Example:** A smart contract platform might conduct regular audits of its contracts to ensure that they comply with data privacy regulations and function correctly. These audits help maintain the integrity and reliability of the smart contract system.

IV. Blockchain Adoption in Enterprises

Blockchain technology, often associated with cryptocurrencies, has demonstrated its potential to revolutionize various industries beyond finance. Enterprises across sectors such as finance, healthcare, and logistics are increasingly adopting blockchain to enhance operational efficiency, ensure data integrity, and drive innovation. Additionally, blockchain offers substantial benefits for small and medium-sized enterprises (SMEs) and startups, providing them with opportunities to scale and compete on a global level. This section explores the transformative potential of blockchain in different sectors, its impact on cost reduction and efficiency, and how smaller businesses can leverage blockchain technology to their advantage.

1. Applications in Finance, Healthcare, and Logistics

1. Finance

Blockchain technology has made significant inroads into the financial sector, offering solutions to enhance transparency, security, and efficiency in transactions and record-keeping.

Real-World Examples:

- **Cross-Border Payments:** Traditional cross-border payment systems often involve multiple intermediaries, resulting in delays and high transaction fees. Blockchain-based platforms like Ripple (XRP) have transformed this process by enabling real-time, low-cost international payments. Ripple's network allows financial institutions to transact directly with one another, bypassing traditional intermediaries and reducing the time and cost associated with cross-border transactions.

- **Smart Contracts for Derivatives:** Corda, developed by R3, is a blockchain platform designed specifically for financial transactions. It supports smart contracts, which automate the execution of agreements and reduce the need for intermediaries. This application is particularly valuable in trading derivatives, where it ensures compliance with contractual terms and reduces the risk of fraud.
- **Decentralized Finance (DeFi):** DeFi platforms like Uniswap and Aave use blockchain to create decentralized financial services such as lending and trading, without traditional intermediaries. These platforms leverage smart contracts to facilitate

transactions, offering greater accessibility and reducing costs associated with traditional financial services.

2. Healthcare

In healthcare, blockchain technology is being adopted to enhance data security, streamline processes, and improve patient care.

Real-World Examples:

- **Patient Data Management:** MedRec is a blockchain-based platform that allows patients to manage their health records securely. By using blockchain, MedRec ensures that patient data is immutable and accessible only to authorized parties. This approach enhances data security and allows for seamless sharing of health information among healthcare providers, improving the quality of care and reducing administrative burdens.

- **Drug Traceability:** Modum uses blockchain to track the supply chain of pharmaceuticals. By recording every transaction and movement of drugs on a blockchain, Modum ensures that products are genuine and have been stored under the required conditions. This traceability helps prevent counterfeit drugs and ensures compliance with regulatory standards.
- **Clinical Trials:** ClincialTrials.io leverages blockchain to manage and verify clinical trial data. The technology provides a transparent and immutable record of trial results, which helps to ensure data integrity and prevent manipulation. This transparency enhances the credibility of clinical trials and accelerates the drug approval process.

3. Logistics

Blockchain's potential in logistics lies in its ability to provide real-time visibility, enhance traceability, and optimize supply chain operations.

Real-World Examples:

- **Supply Chain Transparency:** IBM Food Trust, a blockchain-based platform, is used by companies like Walmart and Nestlé to track the origin and movement of food products. By recording every step of the supply chain on a blockchain, IBM Food Trust enhances transparency and allows consumers to verify the provenance of their food. This traceability improves food safety and reduces the impact of recalls.

- **Smart Contracts for Logistics:** VeChain utilizes blockchain and smart contracts to optimize logistics operations. By automating the execution of contracts based on predefined conditions, VeChain reduces the need for manual intervention and minimizes errors in logistics processes. This approach streamlines operations and improves efficiency across the supply chain.

- **Automated Payments:** TradeLens, developed by IBM and Maersk, uses blockchain to automate and streamline the documentation and payment processes in shipping. By digitizing and automating these processes, TradeLens reduces paperwork, accelerates transactions, and enhances overall efficiency in the logistics industry.

2. Cost Reduction and Efficiency Gains

Blockchain technology offers substantial benefits in terms of cost reduction and efficiency gains for enterprises. By eliminating intermediaries, automating processes, and enhancing transparency, businesses can achieve significant improvements in their operations.

1. Reducing Intermediaries and Transaction Costs

One of the primary advantages of blockchain is its ability to eliminate intermediaries. Traditional business processes often involve multiple intermediaries, each adding their own costs and delays. Blockchain's decentralized nature allows for direct transactions between parties, reducing the need for intermediaries and lowering transaction costs.

- **Example:** In the financial sector, blockchain-based platforms for cross-border payments reduce the need for correspondent banks and payment processors. This elimination of intermediaries leads to faster transactions and lower fees, benefiting both businesses and consumers.

2. Automating Processes with Smart Contracts

Smart contracts automate the execution of agreements based on predefined conditions. By automating processes, businesses can reduce the need for manual intervention, minimize errors, and accelerate transactions.

- **Example:** In the logistics industry, smart contracts can automate the verification of shipment conditions and trigger payments upon successful delivery. This automation reduces administrative overhead and ensures that transactions are executed promptly and accurately.

3. Enhancing Transparency and Reducing Fraud

Blockchain's immutable and transparent ledger enhances trust and reduces the risk of fraud. Every transaction recorded on a blockchain is visible and cannot be altered, providing a verifiable record of activities.

- **Example:** In supply chain management, blockchain enables end-to-end traceability of products. This transparency helps prevent counterfeit goods and ensures that products meet quality and safety standards. By reducing the risk of fraud, businesses can avoid costly recalls and reputational damage.

4. Improving Operational Efficiency

Blockchain technology streamlines operations by providing real-time visibility and automating routine tasks. This efficiency gain allows businesses to optimize their processes and allocate resources more effectively.

- **Example:** In healthcare, blockchain-based patient data management systems reduce administrative burdens and streamline the process of sharing health information. This efficiency improves patient care and reduces the time spent on administrative tasks.

3. Blockchain Utilization for SMEs and Startups

Blockchain technology offers numerous opportunities for small and medium-sized enterprises (SMEs) and startups. By leveraging blockchain, these businesses can gain a competitive edge, access new markets, and enhance their operational efficiency.

1. Accessing New Markets and Opportunities

Blockchain technology enables SMEs and startups to enter new markets and access opportunities that were previously out of reach. For example, blockchain-based platforms can facilitate cross-border transactions and reduce the barriers to international trade.

- **Example:** OpenBazaar is a decentralized marketplace that allows small businesses to conduct transactions directly with buyers around the world. By using blockchain, OpenBazaar eliminates the need for intermediaries and enables SMEs to reach a global audience.

2. Reducing Operational Costs

SMEs and startups often face budget constraints and need to find cost-effective solutions. Blockchain technology can help reduce operational costs by automating processes, minimizing intermediaries, and enhancing transparency.

- **Example:** Provenance is a blockchain-based platform that helps businesses track the origin and journey of their products. By providing transparency and reducing the need for intermediaries, Provenance enables SMEs to reduce costs associated with supply chain management.

3. Enhancing Trust and Credibility

Blockchain technology enhances trust and credibility by providing a transparent and immutable record of transactions. For SMEs and startups, this trust is crucial for building relationships with customers, partners, and investors.

- **Example:** Certify is a blockchain-based certification platform that allows businesses to issue and verify certificates of authenticity. By using blockchain, Certify ensures that certificates are tamper-proof and verifiable, enhancing trust and credibility for SMEs.

4. Leveraging Blockchain for Innovation

Blockchain technology offers opportunities for innovation and differentiation. SMEs and startups can leverage blockchain to develop new products, services, and business models that set them apart from competitors.

- **Example:** Brave is a blockchain-based web browser that rewards users for their attention and privacy. By leveraging blockchain, Brave offers a unique value proposition that addresses growing concerns about online privacy and data security.

5. Enabling Crowdfunding and Investment

Blockchain technology facilitates new methods of raising capital, such as Initial Coin Offerings (ICOs) and Security Token Offerings (STOs). These methods provide SMEs and startups with alternative funding options and access to a broader investor base.

- **Example:** Ethereum has been used for numerous ICOs, allowing startups to raise funds by issuing tokens on the Ethereum blockchain. This approach provides startups with access to capital and allows investors to participate in early-stage funding opportunities.

Conclusion: The Future of Blockchain and Investment Strategies

Blockchain technology, once a nascent idea, has now firmly established itself as a transformative force across various industries, particularly within the financial sector. From decentralized financial systems to innovative investment opportunities, blockchain continues to shape the future of how we store, transfer, and value digital assets. In the final analysis, the future of blockchain is filled with exciting possibilities for innovation, as well as challenges that must be addressed for its sustainable growth. This conclusion will explore key themes such as the sustainability of digital asset investments, blockchain's potential for ongoing innovation, strategies for integrating mining and trading for maximum profit, and the impact of technological advancements on investment opportunities.

I. **Sustainability of Digital Asset Investments: Long-term Viability of Cryptocurrency Investments**

The sustainability of digital asset investments is a critical issue that looms large as blockchain technology matures. Given the significant volatility in cryptocurrency prices, questions about the long-term viability of these investments are frequently raised. While early adopters and investors have profited immensely from the rapid rise in cryptocurrency values, the fluctuating nature of digital currencies such as Bitcoin and Ethereum has led some to question whether these assets represent a stable, long-term investment.

The long-term viability of digital asset investments depends on several factors, including regulatory clarity, technological advancement, adoption rates, and the ability to resolve scalability and environmental concerns. For instance, Bitcoin has been criticized for its high energy consumption due to its Proof of Work

(PoW) consensus mechanism, which raises questions about its sustainability in a world increasingly focused on climate change and carbon footprints. However, the advent of more energy-efficient consensus mechanisms such as Proof of Stake (PoS) presents a more environmentally friendly alternative and could drive greater adoption in the future.

For cryptocurrency investments to remain sustainable, there must also be broader institutional adoption. Recent years have seen increased interest from institutional investors, including hedge funds, family offices, and even publicly traded companies investing in cryptocurrencies like Bitcoin. Institutional adoption lends legitimacy and stability to digital assets, making them a more appealing option for long-term investment portfolios. Governments and central banks, too, are exploring the possibilities of Central Bank Digital Currencies (CBDCs), which could serve as a stabilizing force in the broader digital asset ecosystem.

II. **Blockchain's Potential for Continuous Innovation: How Blockchain Technology Will Continue to Evolve**

Blockchain technology, although still in its early stages, has shown immense potential for continuous innovation. Its decentralized, transparent, and secure nature offers numerous applications beyond cryptocurrency. Blockchain has been applied in industries such as healthcare, supply chain management, real estate, and finance, with the potential to revolutionize how businesses and governments operate.

One of the key areas where blockchain is expected to evolve is in scalability. Early blockchain systems, such as Bitcoin and Ethereum, have struggled with scalability issues, which limit their ability to process a high volume of transactions efficiently. However, new innovations such as Layer 2 solutions and sidechains are being developed to address these issues. For example, Ethereum's transition to Ethereum 2.0, which incorporates the PoS consensus mechanism, is expected to significantly improve its scalability and energy efficiency. Similarly, solutions like the Lightning Network for Bitcoin aim to increase transaction speeds and reduce costs, further boosting the technology's applicability in real-world scenarios.

Another area of continuous innovation is interoperability between different blockchain networks. Currently, many blockchains operate in silos, limiting the ability to transfer assets and information across platforms. Interoperability solutions, such as Polkadot and Cosmos, are working to create an internet of blockchains, where various networks can communicate with each other seamlessly. This will unlock new use cases for blockchain technology and increase its adoption across industries.

Smart contracts and decentralized applications (dApps) represent another avenue for innovation. These self-executing contracts allow for automation in business processes, reducing the need for intermediaries and cutting costs. Decentralized finance (DeFi) has grown rapidly due to the innovation in smart contracts, providing users with services such as lending, borrowing, and yield farming without the need for traditional banks. As more industries explore blockchain's potential for automating processes, smart contracts and dApps will continue to evolve, leading to new business models and opportunities.

Blockchain's role in securing data and privacy is also likely to grow. Innovations like zero-knowledge proofs (ZKPs) and advanced encryption techniques are enabling privacy-preserving transactions that allow data verification without revealing sensitive information. As privacy concerns become more pronounced in an increasingly digital world, blockchain's capacity to provide secure, private transactions will be crucial.

III. Integrating Mining and Trading for Profit Maximization: Strategies for Combining Mining and Trading Activities

As blockchain evolves, one intriguing opportunity for profit maximization involves integrating cryptocurrency mining and trading activities. Mining has historically been a highly lucrative venture, particularly in the early days of Bitcoin and other cryptocurrencies. However, as mining difficulty has increased and energy costs have surged, miners must adopt more sophisticated strategies to remain profitable. One such strategy is to combine mining with trading to maximize returns.

Mining and trading are traditionally seen as separate activities. Miners focus on validating transactions and earning new coins, while traders buy and sell digital assets in an attempt to profit from price fluctuations. However, by integrating these two activities, individuals and organizations can potentially hedge against market volatility and increase their overall profitability.

For example, miners can use trading strategies to sell mined assets at optimal times, capitalizing on favorable market conditions. Instead of immediately selling mined coins, they can hold their assets until market prices rise, allowing them to realize greater profits. This strategy, often referred to as "hodling," can be combined with technical analysis to identify the best times to buy and sell.

Miners can also use futures contracts and options to hedge against price volatility. By entering into futures contracts, miners can lock in a set price for their assets, protecting themselves from sudden market downturns. This provides a stable revenue stream, even in volatile markets, and helps mitigate the risks associated with cryptocurrency mining.

Miners with large amounts of cryptocurrencies can also engage in staking if they operate within a PoS network. Staking allows them to earn additional rewards by locking their assets in the blockchain, thereby further diversifying their sources of income. This combination of mining, trading, and staking creates multiple revenue streams, ensuring that miners remain profitable in both bull and bear markets.

IV. Future Cryptocurrency Market Opportunities: Insights into Emerging Opportunities within the Market

The future of the cryptocurrency market is ripe with emerging opportunities, many of which extend beyond the traditional focus on trading and mining. As blockchain technology continues to mature, several trends are expected to create new avenues for investment and innovation.

One significant area of growth is the development of decentralized finance (DeFi). DeFi is transforming the financial services sector by providing decentralized alternatives to traditional banking functions such as lending, borrowing, insurance, and asset management. These services are built on blockchain networks and use smart contracts to eliminate intermediaries, reducing costs and increasing accessibility for users around the world. As DeFi platforms grow in popularity, they represent a significant investment opportunity for both retail and institutional investors.

Another promising opportunity lies in the tokenization of real-world assets. Tokenization involves creating digital tokens on a blockchain that represent ownership of physical or financial assets such as real estate, stocks, bonds, or commodities. This allows for fractional ownership and increases liquidity, making it easier for investors to buy and sell assets in smaller amounts. Tokenization has the potential to democratize access to investment opportunities, enabling more people to participate in markets that were previously restricted to wealthy individuals or institutional investors.

Non-fungible tokens (NFTs) also present a growing opportunity within the cryptocurrency market. NFTs are unique digital assets that represent ownership of digital art, music, collectibles, and other forms of media.

While the NFT market is still in its early stages, it has already garnered significant attention, with some NFTs selling for millions of dollars. As more industries adopt NFTs for various applications, including entertainment, gaming, and intellectual property rights, this market is expected to grow substantially.

Blockchain-based solutions for supply chain management, healthcare, and data security are also poised for significant growth. These applications leverage blockchain's transparency and immutability to improve efficiency, reduce fraud, and enhance data security in critical industries. As these sectors continue to explore the potential of blockchain, new investment opportunities will arise.

V. **Impact of Technological Advancements on Investment: How Cutting-edge Technologies Will Influence the Investment Landscape**

Technological advancements will play a key role in shaping the future of blockchain and cryptocurrency investments. Emerging technologies such as artificial intelligence (AI), machine learning, quantum computing, and the Internet of Things (IoT) will intersect with blockchain, creating new possibilities and challenges for investors.

AI and machine learning, for example, can be integrated with blockchain to enhance predictive analytics and trading algorithms. These technologies can analyze vast amounts of data to identify market trends, enabling traders and investors to make more informed decisions. Machine learning models can also improve risk management by identifying patterns of behavior associated with fraud or market manipulation, increasing the security and transparency of the cryptocurrency market.

Quantum computing represents both an opportunity and a challenge for blockchain technology. On the one hand, quantum computers could potentially crack the cryptographic algorithms that underpin many blockchain networks, posing a threat to the security of digital assets. On the other hand, quantum-resistant cryptography is already being developed, and quantum computing could ultimately improve the speed and efficiency of blockchain systems. Investors will need to stay informed about these developments, as quantum computing could have a profound impact on the future of blockchain.

The integration of blockchain with IoT devices is another exciting frontier. IoT devices generate massive amounts of data, and blockchain offers a secure, decentralized platform for storing and verifying this information.

Bibliography

- Antonopoulos, Andreas M. Mastering Bitcoin: Unlocking Digital Cryptocurrencies. O'Reilly Media, 2017.
- Bitcoin.org. "Bitcoin Developer Guide." Accessed August 15, 2023. https://bitcoin.org/en/developer-guide.
- Casey, Michael J., and Paul Vigna. The Truth Machine: The Blockchain and the Future of Everything. St. Martin's Press, 2018.
- Crosby, Michael, Nachiappan Pattanayak, Sanjeev Verma, and Vignesh Kalyanaraman. "Blockchain Technology: Beyond Bitcoin.' Applied Innovation Review 2 (2016): 6-19.
- Ethereum Foundation. "Ethereum Whitepaper." Accessed August 10, 2023. https://ethereum.org/en/whitepaper/.
- Franco, Pedro. Understanding Bitcoin: Cryptography, Engineering, and Economics. Wiley, 2014.

- Gensler, Gary. "Cryptocurrencies and Blockchain Technology: The Impact on Global Markets." Harvard Business Review, June 2021.
- Lewis, Danny. Blockchain Basics: A Non-Technical Introduction in 25 Steps. Apress, 2018.
- Mougayar, William. The Business Blockchain: Promise, Practice, and the Application of the Next Internet Technology. Wiley, 2016.
- Narayanan, Arvind, Joseph Bonneau, Edward Felten, Andrew Miller, and Steven Goldfeder. Bitcoin and Cryptocurrency Technologies: A Comprehensive Introduction. Princeton University Press, 2016.
- Nakamoto, Satoshi. "Bitcoin: A Peer-to-Peer Electronic Cash System." Bitcoin.org, 2008. https://bitcoin.org/bitcoin.pdf.
- Preneel, Bart. Advances in Cryptology – EUROCRYPT 2020: 39th Annual International Conference. Springer, 2020.
- Rosic, Ameer. Blockchain for Dummies. John Wiley & Sons, 2019.

- Swan, Melanie. Blockchain: Blueprint for a New Economy. O'Reilly Media, 2015.
- Tapscott, Don, and Alex Tapscott. Blockchain Revolution: How the Technology Behind Bitcoin is Changing Money, Business, and the World. Penguin, 2016.
- Vigna, Paul, and Michael J. Casey. The Age of Cryptocurrency: How Bitcoin and Digital Money are Challenging the Global Economic Order. St. Martin's Press, 2015.
- Wood, Gavin. "Ethereum: A Secure Decentralized Generalized Transaction Ledger." Accessed July 29, 2023. https://ethereum.github.io/yellowpaper/paper.pdf.
- Wright, Aaron, and Primavera De Filippi. Blockchain and the Law: The Rule of Code. Harvard University Press, 2018.

Glossary

1. 51% Attack

A scenario in which a single entity or group gains control over more than 50% of a blockchain network's mining hash rate or computational power. This allows them to manipulate transactions, including double-spending or halting the verification of new transactions.

2. Address

A string of alphanumeric characters used in blockchain networks to identify the source or destination of cryptocurrency transactions. Each address is associated with a private key and is used to send or receive digital assets like Bitcoin or Ethereum.

3. Altcoin

Any cryptocurrency that is not Bitcoin. Altcoins, short for "alternative coins," include thousands of digital currencies like Ethereum, Litecoin, and Ripple. Many offer unique features or improvements upon Bitcoin's model.

4. ASIC (Application-Specific Integrated Circuit)

A specialized hardware device used in cryptocurrency mining, designed to perform a single function—such as solving complex cryptographic puzzles used in Proof of Work (PoW) consensus mechanisms—more efficiently than CPUs or GPUs.

5. Block

A collection of transaction data that is bundled together and verified on a blockchain. Blocks are linked to previous blocks, forming a continuous chain that provides a tamper-resistant ledger of all network transactions

6. Blockchain

A decentralized and distributed digital ledger that records transactions across a network of computers. It operates on principles of cryptography and consensus to ensure that the ledger is secure, immutable, and transparent.

7. Consensus Algorithm

A mechanism that enables a blockchain network to agree on the validity of transactions and ensure the network operates as a single source of truth. Examples include Proof of Work (PoW), Proof of Stake (PoS), and Byzantine Fault Tolerance (BFT).

8. Cryptocurrency

A digital or virtual form of currency that uses cryptographic techniques for securing transactions and controlling the creation of new units. The most well-known cryptocurrency is Bitcoin, but thousands of others exist.

9. CPU Mining

The process of mining cryptocurrency using a computer's Central Processing Unit (CPU). While common in the early days of Bitcoin, CPU mining is now largely obsolete due to the rise of more efficient mining methods like ASIC and GPU mining.

10. Decentralization

A core principle of blockchain technology that involves distributing control across a wide network rather than placing it in the hands of a central authority. In decentralized systems, no single entity can manipulate the system unilaterally.

11. DLT (Distributed Ledger Technology)

The technology underlying blockchain, which allows for the storage and management of data across multiple locations (nodes) in a decentralized manner, making the system resilient to tampering and centralized control.

12. Double Spending

A potential problem in digital currency systems where the same digital token could be spent more than once. Blockchain technology prevents double-spending by ensuring each transaction is confirmed and recorded in a decentralized ledger.

13. Equihash

A memory-hard Proof of Work (PoW) algorithm designed to be ASIC-resistant. It is used in cryptocurrencies like Zcash to make mining more accessible by preventing mining domination by specialized hardware like ASICs.

14. Ethereum

A decentralized blockchain platform known for its smart contract functionality, allowing developers to create decentralized applications (DApps) on top of its network. Ether (ETH) is the native cryptocurrency used to pay for transactions and computational services.

15. Fork

A change or upgrade in a blockchain's protocol. A hard fork creates a permanent divergence in the blockchain, resulting in two separate chains, while a soft fork is a backward-compatible update to the blockchain.

16. GPU Mining

The use of Graphics Processing Units (GPUs) for cryptocurrency mining. GPUs are more efficient than CPUs for mining tasks that involve solving cryptographic puzzles, making them popular for mining altcoins like Ethereum.

17. Hash Function

A mathematical algorithm that converts an input (or "message") into a fixed-length string of bytes. In blockchain, hash functions are used to ensure the security and integrity of transactions by producing unique and irreversible outputs for every input.

18. Hash Rate

A measure of computational power used in cryptocurrency mining. It represents the number of hash operations a miner can perform per second, which directly correlates to the miner's ability to solve cryptographic puzzles and earn rewards.

19. HODL

A term derived from a misspelled word "hold," referring to the strategy of holding onto cryptocurrency for long-term gains rather than selling during market volatility. It is often associated with confidence in the long-term value of cryptocurrencies like Bitcoin.

20. ICO (Initial Coin Offering)

A fundraising method used by blockchain projects to raise capital by issuing new tokens in exchange for cryptocurrencies like Bitcoin or Ethereum. ICOs are similar to IPOs (Initial Public Offerings) in traditional finance but typically offer fewer regulatory protections.

21. Ledger

A database or record-keeping system in which financial transactions are recorded. In blockchain, the ledger is decentralized and distributed across all nodes, providing transparency and security to the network.

22. Liquidity

The degree to which an asset can be quickly bought or sold in the market without affecting its price. In cryptocurrency markets, liquidity refers to how easily tokens can be converted into cash or other cryptocurrencies.

23. Mining

The process of using computational power to validate transactions and secure a blockchain network. Miners are rewarded with newly created coins (in PoW systems) or transaction fees (in PoS systems) for their work.

24. Node

A participant in a blockchain network that helps validate and relay transactions. Nodes can range from lightweight clients that validate specific transactions to full nodes that maintain a complete copy of the blockchain ledger.

25. Nonce

A random or unique number used once in cryptographic communication. In cryptocurrency mining, miners adjust the nonce to find a hash that meets the specific requirements of a blockchain network (e.g., a certain number of leading zeros).

26. Proof of Stake (PoS)

A consensus mechanism that selects validators based on the number of coins they hold and are willing to "stake" as collateral. PoS is seen as a more energy-efficient alternative to Proof of Work (PoW), which requires miners to solve computational puzzles.

27. Proof of Work (PoW)

A consensus mechanism used by cryptocurrencies like Bitcoin. Miners compete to solve complex mathematical puzzles, and the first one to solve the puzzle gets to add a new block to the blockchain and receive a reward.

28. Scrypt

A memory-hard cryptographic algorithm used in some cryptocurrencies like Litecoin. Scrypt is designed to require large amounts of memory, making it harder for specialized ASIC devices to dominate the mining process.

29. Smart Contract

Self-executing contracts with the terms of the agreement directly written into code. Smart contracts automatically execute and enforce agreements when pre-specified conditions are met, without the need for intermediaries.

30. Staking

The process of participating in a Proof of Stake (PoS) blockchain network by holding and "staking" coins to support the network's security and operations. Stakers are rewarded with additional coins for helping to validate transactions.

31. Token

A digital representation of value, utility, or an asset within a blockchain network. Tokens can represent anything from ownership in a company (security tokens) to the right to access a particular service (utility tokens).

32. Wallet

A digital tool used to store, send, and receive cryptocurrency. Wallets can be hot (connected to the internet) or cold (offline for security) and can store public and private keys required for accessing digital assets.

33. Zero-Knowledge Proof

A cryptographic method that allows one party to prove to another that they know a value without revealing the value itself. Zero-knowledge proofs are used in blockchain technology to enhance privacy and security in transactions.

www.ingramcontent.com/pod-product-compliance
Lightning Source LLC
Chambersburg PA
CBHW052143220526
45471CB00004B/1500